A Third Book of 101 School Assembly Stories

A Third Book of 101 School Assembly Stories

London

W. FOULSHAM & CO. LIMITED

NEW YORK TORONTO CAPE TOWN SYDNEY

W. FOULSHAM & CO. LIMITED
Yeovil Road, Slough, Berks., England

Also published by Foulsham:

101 School Assembly Stories

A Second Book of 101 School Assembly Stories

and

A Fourth Book of 101 School Assembly Stories

ISBN 0-572-01411-2
Text & Artwork © W. Foulsham & Co. Ltd. 1987

Printed and bound in Great Britain at The Bath Press, Avon

Contents

Contributors

Harold R. Bowering
Dave Britton
Norman Bury
A. F. Buttery
Angela Cotton
H. K. Dean
Bryan Dodd

T. M. Gannon
G. M. Kitchen
Sue Peirce
Ralph Rickard
Arthur Riley
Harry A. Rose

Illustrated by Nancy Petley-Jones, Peter Kesteven, Colin Grey, Mei Lim

Acknowledgements

Despite every effort it has not been possible to trace the source of all these stories. If an author's copyright has been infringed sincere regrets are tendered.

The Publishers are grateful for permission to use the following stories in this collection:

W. H. Allen & Co. plc. for 'An Outstretched Hand' by Rod McKuen from 'The Rod McKuen Omnibus'

Wm. Collins Sons & Co. Ltd. (Fontana Paperbacks) for 'O God it is easy to love the whole world' by Rita Snowden

J. M. Dent & Sons Ltd for this adaption of 'Suho and the White Horse' by Yuzo Otsuka

John Murray (Publishers) Ltd. for 'Diary of a Church Mouse' by John Betjeman from 'Collected Poems'.

The General of The Salvation Army 1981 for 'Days' and 'Conformity' by John Gowans in 'O Lord'.

TRUE STORIES

Admiral Lord Nelson

Horatio Nelson was quite a slightly built boy, and although he did not enjoy very good health he nevertheless liked having adventures. He also had a very strong sense of what was right and what was wrong.

One cold day in the middle of winter, Horatio and his brother William set off to walk to school, but the road was blocked by snow, and so they returned home. Their father, who was the local vicar, told them that they must try again and give up only if it was absolutely impossible to go on. So Horatio and William set off once more, and William, who was older than Horatio, again wanted to give up. But Horatio said, 'No, remember we promised to try and try again.' They did just this, and finally they got to school.

When Horatio was about ten years old he went to Norwich High School, but in those days children left school when they were still quite young. Horatio joined the navy as a midshipman when he was only twelve years old. He had to learn about navigation and all the other duties of an officer.

Life on board ship was very rough and the discipline was strict, but Horatio enjoyed his life sailing the high seas. At the age of fifteen he went on an expedition to the Arctic, and on one occasion Horatio, who seemed to have no fear, narrowly missed being caught by a polar bear.

Horatio was made a captain at the early age of twenty. He was always looking for a chance to fight the enemy, for at that time

Britain and France were at war. One of Nelson's orders was to capture the island of Corsica from the French. Just when he had reached the shore an enemy shell exploded close to Horatio, missing him by inches. He received bad cuts to his face and his right eye was seriously damaged. In spite of very severe pain he was only absent from his duty for one day. Sadly, Horatio lost the sight of his eye.

Not long afterwards the French general Napoleon took an army to Egypt and conquered the country. Nelson decided he would stop Napoleon's army from getting back home by sinking the French ships. Nelson sailed his warships between the French ships and captured and sank most of them at the famous Battle of the Nile. Horatio was now the youngest Admiral in the navy.

A few years later, at Tenerife, Horatio was shot in his right arm during a war with the Spaniards, and the injury was so serious he had to have the arm amputated. Horatio recovered from his wounds, and as soon as he was able he taught himself to write with his left hand. It was difficult, but he persevered.

When Nelson got back to England he was given a hero's welcome. In a few months he made a complete recovery and returned to his beloved navy once again. He was now in command of a fleet of ships in the Mediterranean.

England was still at war with France, and the French, led by Napoleon, were assembling a large army in readiness to invade England. Napoleon had said, 'If we can control the English Channel we shall be masters of the world.' But to do that he had to defeat the British at sea, and Nelson was *not* going to allow that to happen.

It was October 1805. A fleet of thirty-three ships from France and Spain set out from southern Spain with one aim in mind – the defeat of the British fleet. But Nelson had other ideas!

When he heard that the ships had been sighted he was not worried, for his plans were ready. Nelson divided his fleet into two groups. One group would attack the enemy from one side and the rest of the ships would attack from the other. In this way they hoped to destroy the French fleet before it could send for help.

Nelson sent the famous signal – ENGLAND EXPECTS THAT EVERY MAN WILL DO HIS DUTY. Then the battle started, and Nelson's plan worked brilliantly – many of the enemy ships were captured. Unfortunately, HMS *Victory*, Nelson's flagship, collided with a French ship. One of the French soldiers spotted Nelson on the deck and fired his musket at him. Lord Nelson fell, mortally wounded. Before he died, Nelson asked how the battle had gone. The answer was, 'We have had a great victory.' Nelson replied, 'Thank God. I have done my duty.' The Battle of Trafalgar had been won.

October 21st became known as Trafalgar Day, and it is still celebrated every year in the Royal Navy. Admiral Lord Nelson was a man of tremendous courage. He gave his life for the country he loved.

If you visit Portsmouth you can see HMS *Victory* – our most famous warship – and in London, of course, there is Nelson's Monument in Trafalgar Square.

The Master Potter of Staffordshire

The son of a potter Josiah Wedgwood was the youngest of thirteen children.

Burslem, where he lived, was the centre of pottery manufacture, but the workmen were very poorly paid, receiving only a few pence per week. Their homes were very basic, and had very little furniture. Josiah's mother was a very kind and energetic woman, and she passed these virtues on to her children. She taught them integrity, self-help, self-restraint and perseverance.

Although Josiah attended school, he was able only to learn basic reading and writing there. When he was seven years old, he went to another school, across the moor at Newcastle under Lyme, but on his father's death two years later he was taken away. For the most part, he was self-taught. His father left little property, and Josiah was only to receive twenty pounds when he came of age at twenty-one.

On leaving the school at Newcastle under Lyme, Josiah began to work at the family pottery, now managed by his eldest brother. He had already shown a talent for modelling in clay and cutting out designs in paper, and he soon displayed skill in shaping the clay on the potters' wheels.

11

Unfortunately, however, when Josiah was just over eleven years old smallpox broke out in Burslem, and he caught it very badly, suffering for years from pains in his knee as a result of the illness. Eventually he had to have his leg amputated.

After many weeks Josiah was at last well enough to go back to work, but because of his stiff and painful knee, he had to give up his work at the thrower's wheel and go to the moulder's board, where he originated new methods of manufacture. One of his earliest efforts is still preserved at Burslem and is called 'Josiah Wedgwood's first teapot'.

Josiah was a young man of vision, and he started to manufacture plates, snuff boxes and knife handles in imitation agate, marble and tortoiseshell. His brother was unhappy about this diversification from the usual pots and pans they manufactured, but Josiah insisted, and so he laid the foundation of his future fame. Josiah was the only one of the thirteen Wedgwood children who ever made a name for himself.

In 1752, when he received his father's legacy, he moved to Stoke to begin business with John Harrison, who put up the money for the venture. This arrangement did not last long, however, and Josiah then went into partnership with Thomas Whieldon. This partnership was to last for five years. During this time they made a great variety of articles which were glazed and coloured in imitation of precious stones, which found a large and ready market in the big cities like London.

Eventually the partnership with Whieldon ended, and Wedgwood set up his own

manufacturing factory at Burslem. He was now thirty years of age, but still plagued by his injured knee, and had to spend quite a lot of time in bed, where he studied arithmetic, geography, English literature and art.

Josiah was always trying something new in the art of pottery: he created medallions and ornamental ware, and produced work in reliefs, such as storks and ducks. Business was very good, and the works were expanded. Josiah's fame spread rapidly, and royal patronage was granted to Wedgwood ware when Queen Charlotte ordered a tea service. Josiah was so proud of this order that he superintended all the work himself, not trusting it to an employee. The Queen was very pleased with the tea set and gave him a further order, and also requested that the service should bear the name of 'The Queen's Ware' and that

Wedgwood should be appointed 'Potter to her Majesty.' Soon 'Queen's Ware' became the main pottery of England.

Unable to find a suitable site for the big increase in the size of his factory that trade demanded, Wedgwood found some land a short distance away, near Hanley. This new site he called Etruria, because in the Etruria Valley in Italy they produced fine pottery, which Wedgwood admired.

Josiah was a very good employer to his men, and was always available to hear their grievances. When he tried to hold a public meeting to discuss the question of the road from the Potteries to Liverpool – the main port of shipment for English pottery – the plan to improve the route was initially opposed. But Josiah was insistent, and in time the road was indeed improved. In addition, canals were also built to help in the transportation of the pottery. This cut down on breakages caused by the terrible potholes in the roads over which the pottery normally had to travel.

St Valentine's Day

St Valentine's Day falls on the 14th February. A certain Roman emperor was constantly leading his army of 1000 soldiers into battle. He had no sooner defeated one country than he attacked the next. One day he said to his officers, 'My men have been on leave for almost four weeks. It is time they were sharpened up. Tell them all to report back for duty within four days.'

'But Emperor,' would it not be better to allow the soldiers to stay with their families a little longer?' asked one of his officers. 'They have wives and children whom they love. They are afraid that the next battle may be their last.'

'Afraid?' exclaimed the emperor. 'My soldiers are never afraid! If wives and children are making some of my soldiers – the emperor's soldiers – afraid, then tomorrow I shall issue a decree: From this day, no soldier in the Roman Army shall be given permission to marry. See that my orders are carried out promptly.'

There was one man living in Rome at this time who believed that the emperor's decree was cruel and unjust. 'It is God's will,' said Bishop Valentine, 'that men and women should love one another, that

13

men and women should be free to marry and have families.'

Before long the soldiers heard about the good bishop and started to ignore the emperor's decree by going secretly to see the bishop in order to be married. The day arrived when the emperor's spies heard about these secret marriages. At first they agreed not to inform him, but as more and more soldiers got married they realized that when the emperor did find out what was going on he would not hesitate to kill them all for being disloyal.

They warned Bishop Valentine what they were going to do so that he could flee the country, but the bishop refused to run away. 'I am no coward,' he said. The next day three of the spies craved an audience with the emperor and told him.

'These marriages,' they said, 'Are being sanctified by a Christian named Bishop Valentine.'

The emperor was furious. He shouted in anger: 'Bring this bishop here at once. If what you say is true he will spend the rest of his life in prison.'

Fearlessly and calmly Bishop Valentine told the emperor, 'I obey the Will of God whom I have promised to serve.' He was cast into prison and there he died on 14th February.

After his death he became known as St Valentine. It is said that he keeps watch over all those who truly love.

So, on 14th February boys and girls often send 'Valentines' to their sweethearts. The best are made by hand, but most are bought from card shops, and they are usually greatly treasured. It is also during the month of February that many birds begin to built their nests. Some say it is because St Valentine has been speaking to them.

Douglas Bader

Douglas Bader was only eight years old when he was sent away to a boarding school. His father died of war wounds when Douglas was still at school. He was very good at games, but was not fond of mathematics. Nevertheless he worked hard at this subject and won a scholarship to St Edmund's School, near Oxford.

One day, an officer cadet from the Royal Air Force College at Cranwell came to talk to the boys about the Royal Air Force. Douglas was very impressed, and he decided to try and get into Cranwell College. He worked hard, and passed both the written and medical examinations.

Douglas was thrilled, and in a few weeks he began his training as a pilot. He loved every minute of his flying, and when he was not in the air he was either playing rugby or cricket. He learned very quickly and after only about fourteen hours of flying Douglas was ready for his first solo flight. This went perfectly, and soon he was given his wings at the passing-out parade. By now Douglas had decided he wanted to be a fighter pilot.

Soon he was chosen to be a member of the Royal Air Force display squadron. Thousands of people used to go and watch the aerobatic displays of his team.

One cold December day Douglas was asked by one of the young members of an aero club if he would show them what he could do with his aeroplane. Douglas, not wanting to disappoint the boy, finally agreed. He took off in his Bulldog aeroplane. All went well at first, but then Douglas dived down very low, and misjudged his height above the ground. His aeroplane crashed.

At first Douglas did not feel any pain, but he thought there must be something wrong with his legs – they felt numb. Then he became unconscious. An ambulance rushed him to hospital. Douglas was very seriously injured, and in a great deal of pain. His legs were so badly damaged the doctors were forced to amputate both of them.

Several months later, Douglas was sent to a special hospital where he was fitted with artificial legs. Fortunately, he was a strong young man, and in spite of all the difficulties he kept cheerful. Douglas was absolutely determined that he would walk without a stick or crutches, once he had mastered his 'tin' legs. By the summer he had made an amazing recovery. He could walk without any crutches! Soon he was allowed to go up in an aeroplane again, and after a little practice Douglas was able to pilot the aeroplane himself despite his disability.

A few years later the Second World War began, and Douglas persuaded the Royal Air Force to allow him to continue as a fighter pilot. In a short time he became the leader of a squadron of Spitfires, and he shot down a number of enemy planes. During the Battle of Britain he became one of our greatest fighter pilots and, as the weeks went by, helped to defeat the German air force.

One day in August 1941 Douglas was leading his Spitfires when a number of German aeroplanes were spotted below. They dived down to attack them. A dogfight took place, and some of the German planes were shot down. Unfortunately, during this air battle, Douglas' own aeroplane was hit by a German fighter. He could no longer control his Spitfire. There was not a second to lose. It was time to bale out. Douglas pulled his parachute cord and it opened safely. He drifted slowly down to earth, but with only one of his artificial legs; the other had been trapped in his Spitfire!

He landed in a field and was captured by two German soldiers who took him to hospital. Although he had two broken ribs, Douglas began to think of ways he could escape. With the help of some of the other men in the hospital he tied some sheets together to make a kind of rope. Douglas managed to climb out of the window and quickly got to the ground. A kind Frenchman helped him to a house where Douglas was able to hide.

As soon as the Germans discovered Douglas was missing, they began a search and found him hiding in some straw. Much to Douglas' surprise the Germans allowed the Royal Air Force to drop him a new pair of artificial legs by parachute, but at first they would not let him wear them in case he tried to escape again!

A few days later the Germans discovered that Douglas *was* planning another escape, and so they sent him to a prison called Colditz. Colditz was built like a castle. It had very high walls and all the windows had thick iron bars. The

Germans said it was impossible to escape from Colditz. They were wrong. A few British prisoners escaped and even got back to England – but that is another story.

All the prisoners were very short of food, but Douglas found a way of getting some corn, which he then hid inside his tin legs. When no one was looking he shared the corn among his fellow prisoners. On several occasions Douglas was very nearly caught, but luck always seemed to be on his side. Douglas was a prisoner for three and a half years. When the allied armies reached Colditz and released the prisoners, Douglas and his friends at first found it hard to believe. But it was true. Germany was defeated; the war was over.

One of the happiest days in Douglas' life was the day he led the victory fly-past over London. Douglas was proud and thrilled to be flying his Spitfire again.

Now that the war was over, Douglas was able to travel all over the world helping soldiers, sailors and airmen who, like him, had lost their legs. But others needed help, too. One day he went to see a little boy who had lost both legs in a road accident. His visit helped the six year old boy a great deal. Douglas showed him that he could still live a happy and useful life, even if he didn't have any legs. Douglas even spent the last few years of his life helping the disabled. Quite soon after his death a charity was started in his memory, to help people who are without one, or both legs.

Douglas Bader was a man who, above all else, gave hope to all who suffer misfortune.

Franklin D. Roosevelt

When Franklin Roosevelt was a little boy he loved to go fishing, and as he grew older he came to love sailing, too, especially when the sea was rough. Any kind of boat gave him pleasure. Sometimes he would go as far as he could in a little speedboat and sometimes he would sail gently along in a yacht. Like most other boys, he also played football at school.

In his late teens he went to Harvard University, one of the finest universities in America. Besides studying very hard he kept himself busy. Franklin led the cheers at American football, and he helped to run a club for poor boys in Boston. He was always ready to help when needed.

One day when he was still quite a young man, Franklin took his family on holiday to the seaside. The weather was very hot, and so to cool off Franklin decided to go for a swim. Although it was the middle of summer, the sea was very cold, and when he came out of the water, instead of drying himself straight away he sat down and started to read some letters he had just received through the post.

Soon Franklin started to feel cold and unusually tired, and so he went to bed. The next morning he had a high temperature and his legs started to give him a great deal of pain. The doctor was soon sent for, but Franklin's condition rapidly

grew worse, and in a very short time his legs became paralysed – he had contracted polio.

Franklin was very ill for many months, but throughout all this time he kept remarkably cheerful, and although he was unable to walk, he even helped to teach his young sons to swim by sitting on the edge of the swimming pool and holding out a long pole for them. He was determined that he was not going to be a helpless cripple, and he learned how to move about, first by using steel crutches, and later by using sticks.

A few years later Franklin went to a place called Warm Springs, in Georgia, and he found that the warm waters helped him to regain some of his strength. So delighted was he that he created the Warm Springs Foundation to help other victims of paralysis.

Franklin was a kind man, and he cared deeply for the good of other people. He became well known and soon he was elected to be Governor of New York State. In another few years he was elected to the highest and most important office of all – the President of the United States.

After he had been President for four years he wondered if he should retire. He soon got his answer. He went to a big meeting one day, and when he got to the assembly hall people were shouting, 'We want Roosevelt. Everybody wants Roosevelt. The world wants Roosevelt.' Now he knew that the people wanted him to continue as President. He won the election easily.

Then one day in December 1941 350 Japanese aeroplanes suddenly, and without warning, swooped down and attacked the American fleet at Pearl Harbour in the Pacific. Of course, this brought America into the war. President Roosevelt immediately set to work to put the whole might of America into the fight against Japan and Germany. It took some time to build the thousands of ships, tanks, guns and aeroplanes needed to defeat the enemy, but Franklin worked tirelessly to speed up the work.

During the next few years President Roosevelt travelled the world to meet the allied war leaders, including Britain's Winston Churchill. Sometimes the journeys were dangerous, as for instance when he went by sea to meet Churchill on board the battleship *The Prince of Wales*. The journeys were often long and tiring, especially for someone who was physically handicapped, but Franklin never complained.

Unfortunately, Franklin never lived to see the victory he had worked so hard to achieve, for he died quite suddenly just a few weeks before the end of the war. Winston Churchill said, 'Franklin Roosevelt was the greatest American friend we have ever known.'

Although he was crippled by polio for many years, he also became one of America's greatest presidents.

Gladys Aylward

A little terraced house in London was the birthplace of Gladys Aylward. Her father was a postman. It was not a well-paid job, and so the family had very little money, but Gladys and her sister had a happy home life. When she was thirteen she left school and went to work as a parlour maid.

One night, on her evening off, she went to hear a missionary giving a talk about China. From then onwards, she was determined to go to China herself. The problem was, she did not have enough money to pay her fare. There was only one thing to do, and that was to earn more money. So she decided to work on her day off.

By chance, Gladys heard about a lady missionary in China who was looking for someone to replace her when she retired. Gladys wrote to the missionary and in a few months she got a reply asking her to go out to China to help.

The great day arrived – she had saved enough money to pay her fare. The cheapest way was to travel by train across Europe and then across Russia. It was the longest train journey in the world, much of it over wild and dangerous country. When Gladys finally arrived in China, all she had left was thirty pence. But this did not worry her, she was used to being poor.

The village Gladys was going to was

called Yang Cheng. There were no roads, and the only way of reaching the village was by mule over mountain passes. In the mountains there were bandits, and wolves prowled around at night.

At last Gladys arrived. Yang Cheng was not a bit like the villages in England. It was surrounded by a big wall and all the gates into the village were locked at night. Gladys was shocked by the cruelty of many of the people, but she hoped she could teach them better ways by preaching Christianity. However, the first thing she had to do was to learn to speak Chinese.

The missionary, Mrs Lawson, with the help of Gladys, decided to open an inn where the men who ran the mule trains could stay the night and have a meal. The Chinese are very fond of hearing and telling stories, and they loved to hear the stories about Jesus – Gladys became very good at story telling.

One day she was asked by the Governor of a prison to go and see him. When she arrived at the prison the Governor told her that there was a riot and that the convicts were killing each other. He said his soldiers were too frightened to go in and stop the riot, and then he asked Gladys if she would try. He added, 'You have been preaching that your God protects you, so you will not come to any harm.' Gladys agreed to go in. One of the guards opened the door and she went into the courtyard. A convict rushed up to Gladys waving a chopper in his hand. He stopped in front of her. 'Give me that chopper,' shouted Gladys, 'at once.' To everyone's surprise the man took two paces forward and quietly handed the chopper to Gladys! Then she made all the convicts line up in front of her, and told them that nothing like this must ever happen again.

The Governor was amazed at Gladys' courage, and in a quiet voice he said, 'Thank you, Ai-weh-dah', which means 'virtuous one'. Gladys became known as Ai-weh-dah for the rest of her time in China.

Most of the Chinese were very poor, and some of them could not even afford to look after their children. Some of the children lived by begging and sometimes mothers would sell their children for a few pence. Gladys started to look after some of the unwanted children. As the months passed, more and more children came to be looked after.

Suddenly one day in the spring of 1938 the Japanese bombed the village of Yang Cheng. Gladys had to be pulled out of the ruins and, though badly shaken, she started to help those who had been injured. Gladys knew that shortly Japanese soldiers would arrive. She knew she must lead the children to safety, but there were nearly 100 of them. It was to be a very long and highly dangerous journey over mountain tracks.

When she wanted the children to come to her, she blew a whistle. On and on they went, only resting when they were exhausted. After about twelve days they reached the Yellow River, where some friendly soldiers helped them to cross. At last they were safe from the Japanese. Almost as soon as Gladys and the children had reached safety she became very seriously ill with a fever. The doctor feared she would die, but slowly she recovered and was able to continue helping the poor and orphaned children.

Later in life Gladys started an orphanage on the island of Formosa (now Taiwan) and she spent her last few years working there. Whenever Gladys saw a child in need she was always ready to help.

Her simple faith and wonderful courage will always be remembered, especially by the children she cared for.

Montgomery of El Alamein

Bernard Law Montgomery, who later became Field Marshal Viscount Montgomery of El Alamein, was born in London in 1887. He came from a large family, and when he was very young his father was made Bishop of Tasmania, Australia. Bernard had a very strict upbringing, and when he was old enough he had to help his brothers and sisters in various jobs in and around the house. On Sundays they all went to church dressed in their best Sunday clothes.

The Montgomery family remained in Australia for about twelve years, and when they came back to England Bernard was sent to St Paul's School in London. There he was given the nickname of Monkey because he was small, tough and very quick in all his movements. He was also excellent at games. When he became famous, he was known as Monty.

Bernard soon began to take a great interest in the army, and once he had made up his mind to join, he worked very hard so that he could pass his examinations. He stayed on at school until he was nineteen and then went to Sandhurst, the famous military college. He was made an officer in the Royal Warwickshire Regiment, and soon he was posted to India.

During the First World War he was sent to France, and almost immediately Monty's regiment came under heavy fire from the Germans. The fighting went on for months, and one day Monty was shot whilst leading his soldiers. A bullet passed completely through his body – he had a very narrow escape. As a result of this, he had only one and a half lungs for the rest of his life. In spite of this, Monty made a complete recovery. He was awarded a medal for bravery.

Monty loved the army, and by the time the Second World War began he had become a Major General. Although the Royal Air Force had defeated the Germans in the Battle of Britain, the British Army had still not had a victory. This was soon to change. Winston Churchill, who was Britain's prime minister, appointed Monty to command the Desert Army. As soon as Monty arrived in Egypt he issued this order:

'There must be no more retreat. If we cannot stay here alive, let us stay dead!'

Straight away he began to make plans and began to address his soldiers. He said, 'You do not know me, and I do not know you. We must, and we will, get to know one another. We are going to hit the Germans for six. We are going to fight and kill the enemy. We *will* win.'

The soldiers loved seeing Monty. They felt he was one of them. Every soldier worked as hard as he could to get ready for battle. Soon all was ready. The famous battle of El Alamein began. Monty's plan worked, and the Germans were defeated. They were under the command of Field Marshal Rommel, an equally competent commander, but they were driven back, and in the next twelve months they were pushed completely out of Africa.

Then Montgomery was given the biggest task of all – he was chosen to command the armies for the invasion of Europe. On D-Day, 6th June 1944, the mighty invasion began. It was the greatest sea borne invasion the world has ever known. Over 4,000 ships, over 11,000 aircraft and hundreds of thousands of soldiers took part. They landed in Normandy. Fierce battles raged for weeks. Finally, the Germans were forced to retreat. Monty was made a Field Marshal – the highest rank of all. Almost a year passed before the Germans were finally defeated, with the help of the Americans too, but it was to Monty they finally had to surrender. In only two and a half years he had led his victorious army over 2,000 miles to victory.

When the war was over, Winston Churchill said that the victory of the Desert Army had never been surpassed in the history of warfare.

Montgomery ranks along with the truly great generals of the past. He was a man who had a strong faith in God, and a man who inspired and trusted the men who served under him.

The Story of the Amish Sect

Imagine, if you can, a life without electricity; no television, no radio or tape recorder, no electric iron, no vacuum cleaner, no washing machine or even electric light. Imagine that you have never once been given, or allowed to buy, a toy of any description, never had a ride in a motor car and never had a button on any of your clothes. Imagine that you live in a world where clothes have not changed in 300 years, where all the men wear beards and no woman uses make-up of any description.

You might wonder in what strange, far-away place such people could live. The answer is Lancaster Country, in the state of Pennsylvania, USA, and in many other small farming communities throughout the USA and Canada. We are talking about people of the Amish sect.

Nearly 300 years ago, in Germany, a religious order calling themselves Mennonites were being persecuted and harassed because of their religious beliefs. One day a traveller, returning from the New World of America, told them of a man named William Penn who was leading a holy experiment on the other side of the Atlantic Ocean. It seemed to the Mennonites that here was an opportunity to worship in their own way without fear of persecution. In the late 1600s they set out for the New World and a new way of life.

After a while a group of the Mennonites calling themselves the Amish quarrelled with the rest of the order on the question of 'shunning'. The Amish believed that it was a sin to have anything to do with members of their church who had broken the strict religious rules of the order. They felt that such people should be shunned, so the Amish set up their own communities, enforcing this punishment. Even to this day they still practise 'shunning', although it is very seldom that anybody breaks the rules that have existed since 1700. They believe that they should only marry partners of their own religious persuasion, and they do not believe in a union between church and state.

Although they are farmers they will not use the machinery of the modern world. They farm without tractors or engines of any sort. The only transport they allow themselves is the horse and buggy. Children are encouraged to love the beautiful works of God in nature and they are taught simple reading, arithmetic and writing in all-age ungraded classes. They do not believe in further or higher education, and although the US government has tried to intervene, they insist on children leaving school at the age of fourteen.

So strange are the farms and people of the Amish sect that visitors come from many miles around to see these people who wear old-fashioned hats and bonnets similar to those of the first American settlers. They also come to see the horse-drawn ploughs and the horse and buggy which belong to an age long gone.

It has been estimated that the tourists bring over 100 million dollars to Lancaster County, but the Amish do not receive a penny of this. Instead they are often forced to pack their few simple belongings on to a horse-drawn cart and move away from the material world of the tourists lest their children be corrupted by what they see and hear. They move on to a place where they can farm and live the same simple life that their ancestors lived for 300 years.

They are people for whom the world has stood still, but they believe that theirs is a better life than we enjoy in our crowded cities.

Conqueror of Everest

Mount Everest is the highest mountain in the world. The local people call it 'Chomolunga' which means Goddess Mother of the World. It is 8, 848 metres, 29, 028 ft, high. It was first climbed in 1953 by two mountaineers – Edmund Hillary and Sherpa Tensing Norgay.

Edmund Hillary was born in New Zealand, in a small town not far from Auckland. His love of climbing began when he went with his school on a trip to the mountainous part of the country one day. He also became very interested in bee-keeping, but climbing was the thing he liked doing best. Edmund was tall and very strong and soon be became one of the best mountaineers in New Zealand.

Eventually he had the opportunity to go and climb in the Alps, and finally in the Himalayas. His climbing skill now was becoming world famous.

For thirty years, many mountaineers had tried to reach the top of Mount Everest – the supreme challenge to any climber. Many died attempting to reach the summit. Two men actually got as near as 330 metres from the top. The British decided to make yet another attempt to climb Everest. Colonel John Hunt led the team, which included some of the best mountaineers in the world. Edmund Hillary was one of them.

In February 1953 the British Everest Expedition set off from England, and in early April all the climbers arrived in the Everest foothills. Edmund Hillary met Tensing for the first time, and soon they got to know each other well.

After several weeks of hard climbing across dangerous ice falls and glaciers the team set up their base camp. Now the real climb began. Seven more camps had to be set up. Higher and higher they climbed. Colder and colder it became. Four of the very strongest of the climbers were chosen to try and reach the peak. The first two failed because of bad weather. Now it was Edmund and Tensing's turn.

Edmund and Tensing set off in good spirits. They were carrying extra clothing, sleeping bags, food and oxygen and also a small tent and air mattresses. In a few hours they set up their little tent on a tiny ledge just over 300 metres from the summit. The temperature was a bitterly cold minus 27°C. As soon as they had erected the tent they ate some sardines on biscuits, jam and honey. They were only able to sleep for an hour or two and were very uncomfortable.

At four o'clock in the morning on 29th May 1953 Hillary and Tensing rose from their sleeping bags, made a warm drink and had something to eat, and checked their oxygen masks and cylinders. The sky was clear, although it was still very cold, and so they set off towards the summit. It was 6:30 am. The going was slow, but steady. Nobody had ever climbed as high as this before. Step by step they inched nearer and nearer to their goal. Then one last step. They were on top of the world! It was 11:30 am. Everest had at last been conquered! They shook hands and hugged one another. Edmund took some photographs. They planted flags, including the Union Jack, and then they both ate a piece of Kendal mint cake to celebrate! There was only enough time to spend a quarter of an hour on the summit because their oxygen supply was getting low.

Slowly they made their way down to one of the lower camps and with a sigh of relief collapsed into their sleeping bags. It was a proud and wonderful moment for all the team to know that their attempt had been successful.

The world learned about the first climbing of Everest on the day of our Queen's coronation. Edmund was knighted by the Queen and Tensing Norgay was awarded the George Cross. Edmund was now famous all over the world. He met a great many important people in many countries and was asked to give dozens of lectures about the climbing of Everest.

Since the ascent of Everest, Edmund has been on a number of other expeditions, including an expedition across Antarctica. This was the first expedition to go right across the continent. Edmund and his team were the first men to reach the South Pole, travelling over land, in 46 years. Edmund Hillary has a great affection for the sherpas of Nepal, the small country close to Mount Everest. One of his greatest ambitions was to build a hospital for the sherpas. When sufficient money had been raised in his native New Zealand, Edmund went back to Nepal and helped to build the hospital.

A famous mountaineer was once asked, 'Why does man want to climb great mountains?' The mountaineer replied simply, 'Because they are there.'

The climbing of Everest will always be regarded as one of man's greatest adventures.

Christmas Behind the Wire

This is not a story about animals in a zoo or a wildlife park, but about a group of men in a prisoner-of-war camp. It is a true story.

Christmas should be a time of happiness, of parties, and above all of the family, and a time when a special family is remembered – that family in Bethlehem nearly 2000 years ago. Together with a lot of other men the subject of this story, whom we shall call John, spent five Christmasses in prisoner-of-war camps far from home and family. In a way these Christmasses were a little bit like that first Christmas in Bethlehem: there wasn't much comfort, it was bitterly cold and there was little to eat – all so very different from the kind that all of you are used to.

John's first Christmas as a prisoner was spent in a camp in Poland. He had no presents and no cards. If he and the other prisoners were lucky, they might have had a letter from home written two or three months earlier. However, they made the best of it – they put up home-made decorations in the huts they lived in, and even had a Christmas tree. There was a carol service which had to be arranged without any hymn books, only a Bible.

Christmas dinner that year, 1940, consisted of the usual German soup with a little extra meat and potatoes, but no Christmas pudding or mince pies. Red Cross parcels had just begun to arrive from England; enough for one parcel to be shared by eighty prisoners. John's share of that was a quarter of a packet of tea! Naturally, the prisoners' thoughts turned to home and the hope that by the next Christmas they would be back with their families. From the German barracks came the sound of the carol they all knew as 'Silent Night'.

The next Christmas came, and home seemed even further away. However, in some ways it was for John more like Christmas than the previous year, because he was at a large camp called a Stalag. They arranged a pantomine, a proper church service, letters had arrived and, best of all, so had special Christmas Red Cross parcels in which were tins of chicken and even Christmas puddings.

Two more Christmases passed, and they were still away from home and did not know when or whether they would ever come back. Then came Christmas 1944, which they knew was likely to be the last spent 'behind the wire'. It was very like the others, except that on Boxing Day there was a very big air raid by the Americans. Luckily, no one was hurt. It was one more sign that the prisoners' time in captivity was coming to an end. In fact the day after Boxing Day they were told to be ready to march to the west.

This story has a happy ending, because the next Christmas (1945) was spent at home in England by John.

Although John returned safely to his family and loved-ones after the war, we should never forget all the people in the world who are wrongly imprisoned, especially at Christmas time.

Kings of Speed

To be the fastest man on earth is the dream of many a young person. For both father and son to achieve this ambition has happened only once. Malcolm Campbell and his son Donald both managed this remarkable feat.

When Malcolm left school he spent practically all his money on motorbikes. He even built himself a motorbike, which he used for racing.

Malcolm seemed quite unafraid of danger – he just loved speed. Soon he developed an interest in aeroplanes, and even built himself a small one of those. On its first flight it crashed. Fortunately, Malcolm managed to escape without serious injury.

Then Malcolm turned his attention to motor cars, and joined a racing club at a famous track in Surrey called Brooklands. He now had enough money to buy a fast American car, but because he didn't like its colour, he stayed up all night painting it his favourite colour, which was blue. So he decided to call it Bluebird. Malcolm won the race, so he thought that blue must be his lucky colour. From then onwards he called all his cars Bluebird.

Malcolm became determined to become the fastest man on earth. He finally, succeeded in this ambition when he took his car Bluebird to Pendine Sands in South Wales. Here he became the first man to travel at over 150 miles per hour on land. Shortly afterwards, another famous racing driver called Henry Seagrave broke Malcolm's record. Malcolm decided he would have to build a faster car, and after two years of hard work his beautiful new Bluebird was ready.

As Malcolm began his new attempt at the record there were problems to begin with, and several adjustments had to be made to Bluebird. Then he set off on his fourth run. Malcolm went faster and faster. Bluebird was performing magnificently. When he finished his run the time-keepers rushed up to him with the good news. Malcolm had broken the record again. Some months later, Malcolm's great rival, Henry Seagrave, drove his car even faster, and became the first man to travel at over 200 miles per hour. This car was called The Golden Arrow. Malcolm sent Henry a telegram of congratulations, but resolved that *he* would be the eventual holder of the world record!

For his next record attempt, in February 1931, Malcolm went to Daytona Sands in America. Bluebird roared off and sped down the measured mile. Malcolm had taken the record again! When he got back home, he was knighted by the king. Now he was Sir Malcolm Campbell.

In order to reach the speed of 300 miles per hour, Bluebird had to be redesigned – it needed to be more streamlined. In a few years his massive new Bluebird was ready, and he took it to America again for the record attempt. Soon Malcolm achieved his ambition of becoming the first man to travel at over 300 miles per hour on land.

Although Sir Malcolm was now fifty years of age, he still wanted new adventures. He decided he would also try and be the fastest man in the world on water. His engineers designed a speedboat for the record attempt. Of course, Malcolm called his boat Bluebird, and he became the world's fastest man on water, too. Later he broke the record yet again, on Coniston Water in the Lake District. Then he decided it was time he retired from record breaking.

However, Malcolm's son Donald was ready and willing to follow in his father's footsteps. Like his father, Donald was absolutely fascinated with speed, and he, too, said he was going to break the world land-speed record and the water-speed record as well!

A new Bluebird speedboat was built, and after months of testing it was ready. He took Bluebird to Ullswater and there he became the first man to travel at over 200 miles per hour on water. During the next few years, he kept pushing the record up higher and higher to over 270 miles per hour.

Donald then decided to attempt a new

land-speed record with a new Bluebird car. The attempt was made in America. In seconds the car reached 100, then 200 then 300 miles per hour. Suddenly, when it was travelling at about 360 miles per hour Bluebird shuddered, shot into the air and somersaulted. Miraculously, Donald survived the crash, although he had serious injuries. When Donald had recovered he vowed to try again. Bluebird was rebuilt, and this time the record attempt took place in South Australia. Bluebird streaked down the measured mile at over 400 miles per hour – the record was Donald's!

Sadly, his next attempt to raise the water-speed record was to be his last. In January 1967 Donald's turbojet Bluebird boat raced along Coniston Water. All seemed to be going well. At over 300 miles per hour, without any warning, Bluebird appeared to take off. It made a complete somersault and crashed into the water. Sadly, Donald was killed.

The bravery, determination and skill of Malcolm and Donald Campbell will long be remembered. Truly, they were kings of speed.

Edith Cavell

One rainy day in the village of Swardeston, near Norwich, a little girl was born who was to become famous all over the world for her outstanding bravery. Her name was Edith Cavell.

Edith's father was the local vicar. As a young girl she enjoyed playing in the garden with her sisters. In the summer she also enjoyed racing down the country lanes, and in the winter she skated on the frozen ponds whenever she could. When Edith was still a schoolgirl she once said, 'When I am grown up I am going to do something useful to help people who are unable to help themselves.' Little did she then realize what life had in store for her.

Edith's father thought it would be good for her if she went away to school, and so she attended schools in Kensington, Bris-

tol and Peterborough. At the age of twenty, Edith was appointed a governess and looked after a family of four children. She enjoyed the few years she spent with them. Later she went to Brussels in Belgium, but when her father became ill she returned home to look after him.

It was then she made the decision to be a nurse, which was to change her life. She soon began her nursing training. Being a nurse in those days was even harder than it is now. The hours of work were long and the pay was poor, but Edith loved helping the sick. After a few years she was asked to take charge of a hospital in Brussels. Not long afterwards, a great war began between Britain and Germany, and the Germans invaded France and Belgium, and captured the city of Brussels. The allied armies halted the German advance in a great battle at Mons. Many soldiers were killed and many more were wounded. Edith refused to leave Belgium when the Germans entered Brussels, because she felt it was her duty to help the sick and the wounded. Some of the wounded soldiers were looked after in the hospital where Edith was working.

One day, Edith came into one of the wards of the hospital with three men dressed in civilian clothes. They were really British soldiers in disguise. The Germans were looking all over Brussels for soldiers who had escaped. Edith treated their wounds, gave them something to eat and drink, and found them somewhere to sleep. She knew it was *very* dangerous to hide soldiers, but she also knew she could not hand them over to the enemy. To make matters more difficult, there were

also wounded German soldiers in the hospital, but Edith felt it her duty to nurse and tend all the wounded, whether they were friend or foe.

As time went on, more and more soldiers came seeking refuge. The Germans posted notices on walls declaring that the penalty for helping French, Belgian or British soldiers would be death. This did not stop Edith. Edith and her nurses became known as the Angels of Mons. Often the allied soldiers were hidden in all kinds of strange places, and many of them had very narrow escapes. On one occasion, a British soldier had to jump into bed still wearing his boots when a German officer started inspecting one of the wards! Edith managed to convince the officer that the soldier was quite ill. Fortunately he did not look under the sheets! The German officers were given the nickname 'The Vampires'.

Another soldier had to get hurriedly into a barrel, and Edith just managed to cover him up with a pile of apples before the Germans arrived. One of the French soldiers who was hidden by Edith even managed to get a job dressed in a civilian clothes, working for a circus roundabout. The soldier became a general in the Second World War.

Usually, the soldiers were given secret passwords which they had to use before Edith and her nurses admitted them into the hospital. This was to make sure they were genuine allied soldiers. One day, one of the 'soldiers' arrived who could not tell Edith the password. She knew there was something wrong – this man was working for the Germans. After this, Edith and her nurses had more and more visits by the German officers, and very shortly Edith and some of the Belgians, who had been helping her, were arrested. Very quickly Edith and her faithful helpers were put on trial and were found guilty. They were sentenced to be shot. Edith had expected this to happen. Just before she was shot by a German firing squad, on 12th October 1915, Edith said, 'I must have no hatred or bitterness to anyone.' She added that she just wanted to be remembered as a nurse who tried to do her duty.

After the war Edith Cavell's body was buried in the grounds of Norwich cathedral.

She will always be remembered for her supreme courage and faith.

Abraham Lincoln

Abraham Lincoln was born in a small log cabin in the state of Kentucky, USA, in the year 1809. Abraham's parents were very poor, and the log cabin had only one room 6 metres wide by 5 metres long. When Abraham was only seven years old they moved to Indiana, but soon his mother became ill and died. After a time, his father married again and Abraham's step-mother soon grew very fond of him. She helped Abraham with his schooling.

Although he only went to school for a short time, Abraham was a bright pupil.

Despite the fact that he was quite a serious boy, he also liked having fun and playing practical jokes. But he was always kind to everybody and was very likeable.

Abraham grew up to be very tall – when he was fully grown he measured almost 2 metres in height. He became quite an expert at felling trees with an axe. He was also very strong, and became a champion wrestler. Furthermore, Abraham always believed strongly in the importance of being honest.

At first he did all kinds of jobs; at various times he was a postmaster, a sawmill worker, and an assistant on a local newspaper. A little later, Abraham and another man entered into partnership and opened a shop. In order to start the business it was necessary for both of the partners to borrow some money. The shop did not pay, however, and their debts began to grow. Suddenly, his partner died, but Abraham decided he would work hard until all the money both he and his partner had borrowed was repaid. Abraham was given the nickname of 'Honest Abe'.

Then he decided to study law, and eventually became a lawyer. A few years later he married, and then became greatly interested in the affairs of his country. Soon he was elected to the House of Representatives – the United States parliament.

America was still a young and growing country. The South was very different from the North, where Abraham lived. Many of the rich southerners used black slaves to pick cotton in the fields, to serve in the house and do all kinds of other menial tasks.

The slaves were often cruelly treated by their white masters. When it suited their masters, the slaves were sold, and families were split up. The Southerners wanted to take slavery to the new states in the West, but Abraham was very unhappy about this.

Just at this time, Abraham was elected President of the United States. The refusal by the Southerners to give up slavery caused the American Civil War to begin in 1861. It was to become a bitter war, with the Northern states locked in combat with the Southern states for four long years. Abraham hated war, but he knew that the North must win if the slaves were to be set free.

The most important of the many battles fought in the Civil War was the Battle of Gettysburg. This battle lasted for two and a half days, and about 51,000 men lost their lives. After the battle, the Southern Army was forced to retreat, and from then onwards the North grew stronger and stronger.

A few months later Abraham Lincoln visited the battlefield, and made a very famous speech. He said: 'The brave men who have died at Gettysburg will never be forgotten. They have given our nation a new birth of freedom, dedicated to the ideal that all men are created equal. We will have a government of the people, by the people for *all* the people.'

When the Southern states were finally defeated. President Lincoln declared that all the slaves were to be set free.

On 14th April, 1865, at the end of the war, President and Mrs Lincoln arrived at Ford's Theatre to see a play called 'Our

American Cousin'. They were enjoying the play when, unnoticed, a man called John Wilkes Booth quietly entered the box in which the President and his wife were sitting. Booth suddenly pulled out a revolver and shot the President in the back of the head. Abraham Lincoln slumped forward, mortally wounded. He died a few hours later. His assassin escaped from the theatre, but he was soon hunted down.

America was stunned. Even General Lee, who had been one of the South's most famous generals fighting against Lincoln in the Civil War, was very upset by the assassination.

Lincoln had safely steered America through the most difficult period in its history. He was a truly great president, and will always be remembered as the liberator of the slaves.

The Baby who was Born Twice

The maternity ward in Mexico City's General Hospital had been very busy for several days. So many babies had been born that there were not enough cots in the ward. One baby, José, had been placed in an old metal crib which a nurse had discovered at the back of a storeroom. His mother had been sent home, but he was too weak to be discharged.

On the morning of his third day on earth, the ground beneath Mexico City shook violently. Buildings collapsed in heaps of rubble and thousands of people were buried beneath them. The General

Hospital was no exception. The maternity ward came crashing down with tons of masonry, from the top four floors, on top of it. As the dust began to clear, the horrified survivors gazed at the ruins of their hospital.

Slowly, the shattered city began to stir. Teams of rescue workers were rushed to the stricken areas to begin the slow, agonising task of moving the bricks, concrete and girders in the hope of finding people still alive in the ruins. The rest of the world, shocked by the size of the disaster, sent medical and rescue teams.

For nine days, hundreds worked day and night clearing away debris. Some of those buried in the earthquake were brought out alive, including a few from the General Hospital maternity ward. On the tenth day, it was decided to stop working and bulldoze the ruins flat. There was no point in working any more. After nine days, who could possibly be still alive?

Only José's mother still believed that there was hope. Tearfully she begged the rescuers to continue their efforts a little longer. To quieten her sobs, a four man team made one more attempt. They burrowed deep down through a small gap in the wreckage. After more than an hour, they emerged from the burrow, weeping with joy.

'A baby! Down there! He is alive!'

And so it was that little José was brought from the rubble, crying with cold and hunger. He was black with dust, he had deep cuts on his legs and head and he weighed less than 2½ kilograms – but he was alive.

The doctors tried to explain how he had survived.

'The crib overturned and stopped him from being crushed,' said one. 'A baby is tough and can live off his own resources of fluids. He would not be as afraid as an adult in a dark tomb because it would be like a womb. But ------- ,' he paused. 'Even so, nine days is hard to explain. Who is to say miracles do not happen?'

An elderly Mexican workman who had heard all this, shrugged his shoulders.

'These doctors!' he said. 'What do they know? That little one – he was special. For nine days he lay cradled in the arms of God.'

Michelangelo

Michelangelo Buonarrotti, who lived in Italy during the 15th century, has been regarded by many as the greatest artist that Europe has produced. He was painter, architect and sculptor, but it is perhaps as a sculptor that he would most wish to be remembered. It is said that when he looked at a piece of stone he saw the finished sculpture within, and his task as being only to chip away the stone that imprisoned it.

In the Office of Works in Florence there stood at this time a 5 metre high block of stone that had been seemingly ruined by another artist, who had set out to carve a great figure from it. He had bungled the work so badly that he had hacked a gap between the legs and left the block almost completely mis-shapen. Those in charge had abandoned it, for they doubted that any artist would be able to do anything with it without cutting the stone into much smaller pieces.

Michelangelo, when he saw the figure, immediately felt that here was a great challenge. He measured it, and calculated that he could carve a new figure from it. Then he made up his mind to ask for it. The warden let him have it for nothing, for he could not believe that Michelangelo could make anything of it. But Michelangelo had a vision. Within the stone he saw a young, lithe, powerful David with a sling in his hand. It only remained to reveal him to the light.

In the yard of the Office of Works he constructed barriers round the stone so that no one could see the work as it progressed. Then he built scaffolding to enable him to reach each part with ease.

The result was then, and is even now, regarded as something of a miracle. A man who saw it at the time said that it was so beautifully shaped, and had such grace, serenity and power, that it put all other sculptures in the shade.

It can still be seen today in Florence. Year by year great crowds still gaze and wonder at it. It is a reminder that some people are able to see beauty and nobility where others can only see something ugly and useless.

A Glimpse of the Future

Young Sam Clemens was a lively young-ster – a little more mischievous than the average, perhaps. Certainly more adventurous, and very much at home where there was mud to play in, a tree to climb or paint to splash over himself.

He stood now, uncomfortably in his best clothes, his face unusually clean, facing the strange lady who had descended on their home for the afternoon. She was a very old friend of his grandmother's who had taken the opportunity to call as she was passing through to catch a boat at New Orleans.

Her hand lay clawlike on his shoulder. 'My son, are you saved?' she enquired. Sam puzzled over the strange question. From what should he be saved, or for what? It was a silly question. He wouldn't have been standing there if he hadn't been saved from whatever catastrophe she thought might have befallen him. 'Yes Ma 'am,' he murmured. She peered into his eyes intently. 'I see the Lord has great work for you to do, my boy. Make sure you walk his way.' She nodded her head. 'Great work lays ahead of you,' she repeated. 'Make sure you are worthy . . .'

Years later, when the old lady's visit had long been forgotten, Sam and his brother were both employed on the steam-boat 'Pennsylvania', steaming continuously up and down the Mississippi. They had a sister living in St Louis, and one day Sam took a few day's leave to visit her. It was in her house that he had a strange and disturbing dream. He saw from a distance a metal coffin which had been placed across two chairs. He moved forward to investigate, and found that it was his brother Henry lying in the coffin. On his breast was a wreath of white flowers with a bright red rose in the centre.

Soon after returning from St Louis he had a violent argument with one of the crew, and as a result left the boat. Within two days he had found employment on another boat travelling upstream behind the *Pennsylvania*.

It was at one of the riverside towns that he heard some terrible news. His brother's steamboat had blown up just outside Memphis – 150 had died. Sam rushed to the scene to find his brother alive but with horrendous injuries. For a week Sam hardly left his brother's bedside, but despite all the devoted nursing and care, Henry died. Utterly exhausted by his long vigil, Sam fell asleep. When he awoke he found his brother's body had already been removed. Wearily, he stood up to go and look for it. He was directed to a room down a long passage. He opened the door, then stood in shocked amazement – his brother lay in a metal coffin placed across two chairs just as he had seen in his dream. The only difference was that there were no flowers. As he stood there, the door opened and an old lady entered. She tenderly placed a wreath of white flowers on his brother's breast. She paused, and as Sam looked on in wonder, she took a red rose and placed it in the centre of the wreath . . .

But why the strange glimpse into the future that he had been given? Could it be that in some strange way it helped to change the direction of Sam's life and point him to the road he was to follow for the rest of his days? Was that old lady right, perhaps?

Sam went on to become America's best-loved writer. He changed his name to Mark Twain, and during his lifetime brought amusement and pleasure to millions. His commonsense observations on life must have given many many people comfort and reassurance.

The Fox

For years, the tiny English village had petitioned the local council not to turn one of their most beautiful valleys into a municipal rubbish dump, but they had failed. Day after day, lorry after lorry emptied their loads of suburban refuse where once primroses and cowslips had bloomed and rabbits had frolicked.

One wintry November day, as the rolling mauve-black clouds threatened rain, two of the villagers took the lane that led to the site to see how far the work had progressed. They crossed the stile and there, between the beech woods, stretched mountains of the most assorted rubbish imaginable. Broken armchairs lay amidst soap packets and discarded toys. Arms and legs from display windows stuck grotesquely skyward from beds of newspaper. On the far side the two friends could see a group of men working. They turned their backs on the dump and made for the woods at the side of the valley, as yet untouched.

Some half an hour later their attention was aroused by a poignant cry: a piercing sound at one moment, low and whimpering the next. An animal was in trouble. They followed the sound. Along a barbed wire fence they found a young fox with one of its legs caught in a trap. The more the animal tried to free itself the tighter the noose grew. The leg that was caught was already red with blood. The villagers stood feeling quite helpless. They wanted to help, but surely the frightened animal would attack if approached? They were a long way from the nearest house. The only people who might be able to do something were the men at the council rubbish dump. It didn't seem very hopeful, but the two friends decided to ask.

One stayed to mark the place, and the other made his way back to the dump. Halfway up was a kind of rough shelter. He knocked. A huge man came out. The villager explained his errand. The workman did not answer, but went back into the hut for a tool, and then led the way down the rubbish pile.

The fox was still there, writhing in pain. The man nodded to the villagers to stand well clear. Then, crouching down, he began to talk to the fox softly; coaxing it as if it were a small child, asking it to be still and quiet.

The two villagers watched fascinated as slowly the fox calmed and became still, its eyes looking up into those of the burly man. Slowly but deliberately he reached down with his wire cutters and cut the noose. The fox continued to stand there, with a look of trust. The man stood up. 'Go,' he said. The fox moved a couple of paces and looked back, then bounded into the undergrowth. Within two seconds it was gone.

They thanked the workman and went on their way. They hoped perhaps they might see the fox again, but, of course they didn't.

The implicit trust that a wild animal had in a burly rubbish disposal man was something they felt to be beautiful. If only in our inner struggles we could learn that to fight makes the situation worse. When we are quiet and still we are ready to be responsive to the help that will surely come.

Henry

Henry loved gardening, and even by the age of twelve he was growing vegetables in his parents small garden, and selling them from door to door to make some pocket money.

When he left school he worked in his father's brickyard, but he still kept on growing and selling his vegetables; packing in as much work as possible between getting up at 4 o'clock in the morning and going to bed late at night. He did so well selling vegetables that he was able to buy an interest in his father's brick business, as well as setting up a new company to grow, process and bottle horseradish 'ready to use'. This was over 100 years ago and Henry's horseradish must have been one of the first ever convenience foods.

New products were added, such as celery sauce and pickles, and Henry's business made great progress. But a financial crisis was sweeping America in the 1870s, and Henry was made bankrupt. His family were penniless, with no money even for food for his wife and children.

Yet, in that depressing period, Henry made a note in an exercise book of the names of all the people to whom he owed money when he went bankrupt, marking on the cover the letters M O – moral obligations.

Friends rallied round and helped the family, and it was not long before Henry felt he wanted to start up another business. Unfortunately, as a bankrupt the law prevented Henry from having a business of his own – so he formed a company using the names of his brother John and cousin Frederick.

Henry and his partners worked hard and the business prospered. His fight back to respectability had been hard, but it never affected his compassion for others. He helped to feed down-and-outs, to improve social conditions, and to follow the teaching of the church.

Out of the profits that he made Henry gradually paid back all the money owing to the people whose names were in his moral obligation book, even though he had no legal obligation to do so. When he finally won his discharge from bankruptcy, Henry was able to use his own surname, and the business of H. J. Heinz was registered.

Nowadays, Heinz is a household name, but next time you have beans on toast or a bowl of soup, remember how the famous man fought back and achieved success, without giving up and by not forgetting his moral debts to others.

Jonathan

'Please reverse, I think we passed an injured bird.'

A tiny inert body lay just on the edge of the road. His long tapering swallow's wing had been brutally chopped off, apparently by the overhead wires. Craig picked him up and examined him. A leg was broken; but he was warm. A glazed eye slowly opened; he was alive, too.

It seemed impossible that he could live for long, but we had to give him a chance. A shoe box lined with straw became his bed. We left him for the night, half certain that we would find him dead in the morning.

But not so. Next morning our little patient was attempting painfully to manoeuvre himself about his box using one leg and the stump of one wing. He looked quite determined to live. Our biggest problem was how to feed him. We had discovered now that he was a red-breasted swallow, and swallows feed on the wing. He did not know how to peck for food. After trying to teach him unsuccessfully, Craig had a good idea. Taking a little egg yolk in one hand he 'flew' the bird towards it. On the second try Jonathan, as he was now named, got the idea and grasped it with his beak. Feeding three times a day in this manner become routine.

After a week he was getting himself round his box without tending to roll over on his side, and he had learned to take water from a tin. We greatly admired his courage. In the weeks that followed, he was fascinating to watch. We built him a bigger wooden cage with perches and pieces of driftwood. He learned to climb aboard the driftwood and to maintain his balance. The perches took a little longer. His leg seemed to have healed itself. Now he could walk – after a fashion. He also learned to peck food. Was he the only pecking swallow in existence?

His wing began to grow, but never reached its former glory. He could take long hoppy flights from perch to perch of the bigger and bigger cages that we built for him, but he was never able to fly again. That settled our greatest anxiety concerning him; whether to let him go. It was clear that he would never be fit enough again to survive in the wild.

He seemed happy where he was. He sang a great deal, and his repertoire widened greatly. In fact, we had never heard such a variety of song from one bird. We suspected he imitated birds he heard outside, or even made up his own little tunes. It was delightful to hear. When he had lived with us for about eighteen months we extended his cage so that it jutted out beyond the window into the open air.

One day some time later, as we stood outside, a formation of red-breasted swallows approached. We had never seen them in that area before. They circled several times crying aloud and then flew over Jonathan's cage. It seemed difficult to believe it was just a coincidence. Almost a week later this happened a second time, but there were more swallows and their cries were louder. Jonathan seemed unmoved. He just sat on his perch, head on one side, and watched.

Next morning we found him lying dead in his cage. It had been a privilege to know him. We like to believe that now, with his swallow friends, he flies in skies free from telephone wires in boundless freedom.

Louisa Alcott

Once there were four little girls who lived in a big, bare house in the country. Although they were very poor, they were still happy, because they were very rich in everything except money. They had a wonderful, wise father, and a lovely, merry, kind mother. They also had all the great green countryside to play in. There were dark, shadowy woods, and fields of flowers, and a river. And there was a big barn.

One of the little girls was named Louisa. She was very pretty, and ever so strong; she could run for miles through the woods and not get tired. She also like to study, and thought interesting thoughts all day long.

Louisa sometimes liked to sit in a corner by herself, and write thoughts in her diary: She liked to make up stories, and sometimes she made verses. All the little girls kept diaries.

When the four little sisters had finished their lessons, and had helped their mother wash up and sew, they used to go to the big barn to play; and the best play of all was theatricals. Louisa liked theatricals better than anything.

They made the barn into a theatre, and the grown-up people came to see the plays they acted. They used to climb up on the hay-loft for a stage, and the grown-ups sat in chairs on the floor. It was great fun. One of the plays they acted was *Jack and the Beanstalk*. They had a ladder from the floor to the loft, and on the ladder they tied a vine all the way up to the loft, to look like the wonderful beanstalk. One of the little girls dressed up to look like Jack. When it came to the place in the story where the giant tried to follow Jack, the little girl cut down the beanstalk, and down came the giant tumbling from the loft. The giant was made out of pillows, with a great, fierce head of paper, and funny clothes.

They also acted *Cinderella*. They made a wonderful big pumpkin out of the wheelbarrow, trimmed with yellow paper, and Cinderella rolled away in it, when the fairy godmother waved her wand.

Another beautiful story they used to play was *Pilgrim's Progress*; if you have never heard it, you must be sure to read it as soon as you can read well enough to understand the old-fashioned words.

Louisa loved all these plays, and she made some of her own and wrote them down so that the children could act them.

But above all Louisa loved her mother and, by and by, as the little girl began to grow into a big girl, she felt very sad to see her dear mother work so hard. She helped all she could with the housework, but no-

thing could really help her tired mother except money; she needed money for food and clothes, and someone grown up to help in the house. But there never was enough money for these things, and Louisa's mother grew more and more weary.

Louisa came to care more about helping her mother and her father and her sisters than about anything else in all the world. And she began to work very hard to earn money. She sewed for people and wrote stories for the papers. Every bit of money she earned, except what she had to use, she gave to her dear family.

Every year she grew more unselfish, and every year she worked harder. She liked writing stories best of all her work, but she did not get much money for them, and some people told her she was wasting her time.

At last, one day, a publisher asked Louisa, who was now a woman, to write a book for girls. When she thought about the book, she remembered the good times she used to have with her sisters in the big, bare house in the country. And so she wrote a story about that.

When the book was written, she called it *Little Women*, and sent it to the publisher.

The little book made Louisa famous. It was so sweet and funny and sad and real, – like our own lives – that everybody wanted to read it. Everybody bought it, and much money came from it. After so many years, little Louisa's wish came true: she bought a nice house for her family; she sent one of her sisters to Europe, to study; she gave her father books; but best of all, she was able to see to it that her beloved mother, so tired and so ill, could have rest and happiness. Never again did the dear mother have to do any hard work, and she had pretty things about her all the rest of her life.

Louisa Alcott, for that was Louisa's full name, wrote many beautiful books after this, and she became one of the most famous women of America. But I think the most beautiful thing about her is what I have been telling you: that she loved her mother so well that she gave her whole life to make her happy.

George Herbert and the Carter

The poet George Herbert was, as a young man, a fashionable courtier at the court of Queen Elizabeth I. Then, when barely thirty years of age, he found the life of a courtier empty and meaningless and forsook this colourful existence for the simple life of a clergyman in the small parish of Bemerton. Though he had said goodbye to the fine clothes he had once worn at the court, and changed them for the sober black of a parish priest, he remained very fastidious and neat in his dress.

He was a conscientious man, much loved by the parishoners on whose behalf he worked hard. The only recreation he allowed himself was his music, and he regularly visited a group of friends to join with them in playing the music he loved.

One day he was riding along the road out of Bemerton for just this purpose, when he met a heavily laden cart going up a steep hill. The carter, a large rough-looking man, was shouting and beating his miserable, tired old horse most cruelly.

Seeing that the horse was in considerable distress, Herbert told the carter to stop immediately or he would kill his beast and be worse off than before. He was met with a string of oaths from the carter, a few more blows at the unfortunate animal and the cart barely moved. As the cart came to a halt, I have little doubt that the carter then said something like, 'Now look what you've done.' But George Herbert was a very practical man and one who would never let himself be put off doing what he knew to be right. So he firmly told the carter to come down and, like him, to put his shoulder to the wheel of the cart and give the horse some real help. He then took off his fine black coat and started pushing. The result was that between them, they enabled the heavily laden cart to reach the top of the hill. Then, with a parting word to the carter not to ill-treat his horse in the future, he put on his coat, mounted his own horse and rode on.

When he got to the house where he and his friends were to make music, he found them anxiously awaiting him, for he was rarely late and they feared that some accident might have befallen him. They were also very astonished that the usually very well-dressed Mr Herbert was somewhat dishevelled and looked rather hot.

He let them have their fun at his expense for a few moments and then told them exactly what had happened. He finished by saying that he would have counted himself a poor kind of man and a worse Christian if he had not followed up his well-deserved rebuke to the carter, with all the practical help it was in his power to give.

The Fortress Church

The preacher pointed to a pile of bricks beside the road. 'Had you come last week I could have shown you a fine example of a Victorian church. It was a particularly beautiful one. It stood just there.' he said. As if to emphasize his message a bulldozer careered round the corner, ploughing through the rubble. Afterwards, all that remained was a cloud of dust. And one choking preacher.

In the sixteen years since he came to one of Britain's grimmest inner-city areas, he has lost seven of the nine churches originally under his care. Two were burned to the ground, two more stripped of their lead roofs, and the rest demolished after persistent attacks by vandals. The latest was his favourite. But after its stained glass windows had been repeatedly smashed, its doors axed and walls daubed with paint and its contents stolen, the Church of England signed its death warrant, unable to keep up with the cost of repairs. The preacher, not for the first time, had fought and failed. But you get used to that. The thing is not to be beaten.

If the vandals would insist on wrecking his churches, he decided, he would build one that was vandal-proof. So, in 1976, after much fund-raising and to his own design, the most unusual church in Britain was born.

It is affectionately known as The Fortress Church. It is built of brick, and has no windows on the ground floor. There is grating over the skylight and a sophisticated alarm system. It is also sited – intentionally – next to a police station.

On the wall a poster proclaims: '*This church is for sinners only*'. 'That's because people tend to think church is only for good people. Wrong. It's for everyone.', the preacher explained. His church is his way of fighting back against the helplessness and hopelessness that often exists in deprived inner-city areas.

He has learned that he must stand firm and take whatever is thrown at him. Even when that means personal attacks and abuse. Or having the tyres of his car slashed. Or the vicarage broken into.

He says bluntly, 'Too many churches are scratching people where they don't itch,' 'I remember reading once: "Find a hurt and heal it, find a need and fill it." In our city we have.'

At first The Fortress Church had a Sunday congregation of just twenty. These days it is at least 360, most of them youngsters.

Perhaps it is because services are informal that they cram themselves in. Or because humour, music and drama are high on the agenda. Or perhaps it's because they know they'll be spared a lecture on the unpleasant realities of the city around them.

Inside The Fortress Church a handmade placard hangs on a nail. Three words are printed boldly on it. *Love One Another.*

Uncle Bob

Albert was twenty years of age and was approaching the end of his two years' National Service. He was in charge of an office department in a large military hospital in the south of England. He had two stripes on his arm, and thought he knew it all.

He had his first meeting with death at that hospital. Quite a few patients, of course, died there and he had interviewed many of these when they were admitted. But they were just names on cards and only vague memories to him. The first time he saw a dead body was when a soldier collapsed at the barracks in the nearby town and was brought to the hospital already dead. All Albert saw to begin with was the pair of army-issue boots poking through the curtains round the trolley on which the man was lying. All the formalities were quickly dealt with and he was taken to the mortuary.

That should have been the end of the matter for Albert but, as it happened, he was the duty N.C.O. that weekend. This meant that he had to stay at the hospital all weekend and be available to deal with anything concerning the office side of the hospital work. On the Friday afternoon he was told that the niece of the soldier who had died was coming, with her husband, to see the body the following day and he would have to attend to them. Albert was taken down the path beneath the trees to the quietest corner of the hospital grounds to the mortuary, shown which key opened the door, and was shown exactly where the body was and how to uncover his face. Albert was shaking a little when he went out into the fresh air again. One or two things troubled him. How could someone travel so far to see something so unpleasant? What would he say to them? What would their reaction be? What would they say to him? He was embarrassed.

The wait for their arrival seemed like years, but when the time finally came Albert met them and took them slowly to the mortuary. It was a slow walk, not from any respect for the dead on Albert's part, but because of his reluctance – like someone expecting a painful visit to the dentist, or a schoolboy reporting to his head teacher.

When they went into the mortuary Albert led them to where their relation lay and, knowing what they were about to see, gingerly uncovered the face, doing his best not to look. What happened next came as a complete surprise to Albert. He heard the lady lightly clear her throat and, as Albert glanced at her face, noticing the tears in her eyes, she said, 'Isn't he lovely?' and she bent down and gently kissed him on the forehead. Her husband quietly murmured his agreement.

After a short time they both turned to Albert, smiled and thanked him for his trouble, and he felt a lump in his throat.

As they walked silently back to the hospital Albert felt embarrassed again, but this time it was from shame for his earlier feelings.

The lady and he had both looked at the

same body, and yet they had seen two entirely different things. What Albert had seen was a rather fat, discoloured face. She had seen the man who brought her presents when he visited her family, who sent her birthday cards, who played games with her and took her on outings. She saw her 'Uncle Bob' whom she loved. She saw the person, Albert saw only the body.

'Don't judge a book by its cover', is a well-known saying. Although it can apply to anything, most of all it applies to people. Don't judge people by how they look. An ugly person can be beautiful inside, just as a beautiful person can be really unpleasant. Look for, and find, the person inside.

The King's Letter

Karen Blixen farmed a coffee plantation in Kenya, Africa, in the 1920s. She was a very good shot with a rifle, and on one occasion she had to shoot a lion which was terrorizing her workers. She sent the handsome skin to the king of her home country, Denmark. She valued the letter from the king she received in reply greatly, and kept it in the pocket of her khaki trousers as she went about her work. Karen was very well liked by her African farm workers and is remembered by them with affection to this day. The following story gives some idea why.

A clearing was being made in the forest for new coffee planting, and Karen rode out on horseback to inspect it. Shortly before she arrived on the scene a sad accident had occurred. A young man named

Kitau had been unable to get away quickly enough when a big tree fell, and his leg had been smashed. He was in great pain. Karen sent off a runner to ask for the car to be brought so that he could be taken to the hospital. In the meantime she knelt beside him, feeling helpless to ease his pain and knowing that it would be a long wait before the car came. Kitau groaned, 'Help me, Msaba, help me!' Although she kept morphine at her house for such emergencies she had no medicine with her. She groped in her pockets, she hardly knew what for, and came across some sugar lumps she kept to give to children. She placed one on Kitau's tongue. His moans immediately became less dreadful. He visibly relaxed. But when the stock of sugar came to an end he began to wail and writhe again and to ask, 'Have you got no more, Msaba?'

Once more she felt in her pockets and this time she felt the king's letter. 'Yes, Kitau,' she said, 'I have something more, something very special, a letter from a king! A letter from a king in his own hand will take away all pain.'

At that she laid the letter on Kitau's chest, while at the same time trying to believe that it would help. Almost at once the distorted look of pain on the young man's face cleared and he relaxed.

'Yes,' he said, 'It is very good.'

When the car came, Karen sat in the back holding the letter in position. Even in the hospital she continued to hold it until he was on the operating table.

When Kitau was better and back at his work on the farm, the rumour spread that this 'king's letter' had miracle-working power. People came to ask to borrow it when a child was ill or an old person dying or when a woman was giving birth. Karen put it in a leather bag with a leather strap so that it could be worn round the neck. For years it was greatly used.

Sadly, after some sixteen years Karen had to leave Africa. She took the King's letter with her. By that time it was brown, stiff and dirty. A remarkable document, it had little if any value in itself but was a testimony to the power of faith to overcome bodily weakness and pain, and perhaps even more, a testimony to the respect and love felt for a woman who cared for people.

Dan Vinson

Who are the loneliest people at Christmas time? A salesman by the name of Dan Vinson asked himself this question many years ago. At first he decided that men and women in our prisons must be the loneliest people during the Christmas season. But, on thinking deeper, he came to the conclusion that the children of prisoners must be even lonelier. The result was a unique project.

Since 1943 Dan Vinson, of Oklahoma in America, has sent out millions of Christmas presents to these children without accepting a single cash contribution.

'We haven't done a thing until we give a part of ourselves,' Vinson says. And that is what he asks – and receives – from hundreds of people in all walks of life. Volunteers sort out and package well over a million toys each year, which have been donated by businessmen everywhere.

The children who benefit have never heard of Dan Vinson; he does not want them to know he exists.

'A child wants a Christmas present from someone he loves,' Vinson says. 'That's our basic idea.'

Each year Vinson visits and corresponds with thousands of convicts and wardens, who have heard of him by word of mouth alone. Vinson sends each one a list of twenty-one toys. The imprisoned father or mother checks the present they want, volunteers package the selections and pass them to the parent, who re-addresses the package to their son or daughter. The present, then, is actually from the child's father or mother.

One of Dan Vinson's favourite sayings is the summary of his philosophy:

'A man never stands so straight as when he stoops to help a child.'

Who's a Failure Then?

You have probably read, or have been told, many stories about people who started their lives as members of poor families, but who worked hard to become world-champion sportsmen and women, famous politicians, rich business tycoons or stars in show business. Well, here is a story about failure – or is it?

In the middle of the last century, in Holland, a baby boy was born. His father was a clergyman and a very respected member of the community. The boy, however, was not popular and not very likeable, being unattractive both in looks and temperament. He would make friends, but then would lose them very quickly. He also had terrible fits of depression.

His first job, when he was seventeen, was with a firm selling pictures and books. He had the job of packing them in boxes for delivery, but he lost the job when he fell out with his employers. He fell in love with his landlady's daughter, but he found out she was already engaged.

Then he became a French teacher at a private school in England, and one of his jobs was to collect the fees from the pupils' parents. He was sacked when he failed to get the money. After a short time as an apprentice in a bookshop, he decided to become a minister. In order to do this he needed to go to university, but the studies were too difficult and he left.

He decided to become a preacher anyway, and the religious people who took him on sent him to a very poor part of Belgium. There he devoted all his time, and even his belongings, to the poor. He lived as the poor lived. This did not please those who had sent him there, however. They thought he was eccentric – rather odd – and he was dismissed.

By this time he was twenty-eight years old. He had failed at everything he had

tried. There were times when he became very depressed, and no wonder. Every time he got into difficulty he had to call upon either his father or his younger brother for help. Even as a grown man he was unable to do anything correctly.

It was his brother who suggested he become an artist. Although he had enjoyed painting and drawing since he was a boy, he had never had any proper lessons. So he attended painting classes but, because of his work, he was soon thrown out. He did become a painter, but his work was often laughed at. His brother would send money regularly to help support him, and he sold some of his pictures for a few francs to buy more paint.

He still suffered from fits of depression. In fact, in one of his fits he cut his own ear off. In another, he shot himself in the chest and died shortly afterwards. He was thirty-seven years old.

Since his death a film has been made of his life, a pop song has been written about him and he has been the subject of many books. His paintings sell for many thousands of pounds. His name was Vincent Van Gogh.

The point is this: often you will try your level best and you will fail to achieve your goals; you will do what you think is right and people will scorn you; you will do your best work and it will not always be appreciated. But, perhaps, it isn't you who is wrong, after all. Perhaps it is them! Sadly, in Vincent's case, it was only after his death that people realized the genius of the man who had once been considered such a failure.

The 'Bone Hospital'

In the 1930s a man and his wife were working among African people in the far south of what is now Zimbabwe. Matabeleland, for that is the name of the area, was and still is, very poor. The land is semi-desert, sand, scrub and cacti. There it is scorchingly hot by day and cool, almost cold, at night. The people live a precarious life, scratching poor crops of maize from the soil in years when there is rain, and keeping a few gaunt cattle.

Fifty years ago, the people were in many ways even poorer than they are today, because malnutrition was common, disease took root and rapidly spread. Measles or even the common cold could kill hundreds in the course of a month.

Mr and Mrs Bentley had a small house among the people they had come to help. They felt, not surprisingly, that their job was enormous and they were too small for it. They had a young European nurse and a few semi-skilled African nurses to help them, but that was all. Between them they tried to run a school under a tree, and a church and a clinic in a few huts made of poles and mud. A modern brick hospital with proper sanitation was desperately needed, and as time went by the need grew ever greater as their medical work became known, and people brought their sick relatives from many miles around to be cured by them.

A hospital, then. They needed a hospital, and there seemed to be no way by which they could raise the money to build and equip one. The patients paid a little fruit or a few eggs for treatment. They had no money. The solution to the problem came suddenly and quite unexpectedly and, as they believed, in answer to prayer.

Money did not shower from heaven. Indeed, the doctor's eyes were opened to a source of finance that lay close at hand but as yet unrecognised and untouched.

One day, Dr Bentley was walking along a bush path when his attention was drawn to the bones of a young antelope, wiped clean by vultures, lying to one side. A common enough sight in a desert area. But Dr Bentley felt a sudden excitement. He remembered reading only a short time before in a South African newspaper that bones were increasingly valuable as a source of phosphate in fertiliser. Bones were worth money! And around him in the bush were mountains of them. He devised a plan. Every patient would be asked in future to bring a bundle of bones to the hospital in payment for treatment. When they had a large pile they would take them 100 miles to the nearest city for sale. The idea was so sound, they could even start designing a hospital straight away.

The plan worked wonderfully. In exchange for lorry-loads of bones came building materials, cement, timber and tiles. All the building was done voluntarily by local men and women. All the bricks were made on the site. After four years, the hospital, with fine large wards, an out-patients department, a dispensary, and staff housing was completed and equipped.

Today, twice the size, it is still serving the neighbourhood, and it is still known as the 'Bone Hospital'. It stands as evidence that if you look hard enough you may find a way round the most difficult obstacle in the most unlikely place. And it may be that the answer to your need is, like the bones, close to you, but unrecognised.

Winston Churchill – Man of Destiny

Born in a beautiful Palace in the heart of Oxfordshire, Winston Churchill was to become one of the greatest Englishmen in history.

The most famous of his ancestors was John Churchill, who became the first Duke of Marlborough. Winston Churchill went to Harrow School, one of the best-known schools in England. During his last few years at school he became more and more certain that he wanted to be a soldier, and when he was nineteen he joined the army.

The chance for adventure soon came, and he took part in the famous Charge of the Lancers at Omdurman, South Africa, during the Boer War. Shortly afterwards Winston became a war correspondent for *The Morning Post* and was captured by the Boers, but he soon made a dramatic escape. Eventually he arrived safely back in England.

The following year Winston became a member of parliament, and during the next twenty years he held many important posts in the government of the day, including that of First Lord of the Admiralty – the top post in the Royal Navy. He knew that Germany was preparing for war and he worked hard to make sure that Britain had a powerful fleet of ships that would be ready for action when the war came. The Germans were unable to destroy British sea-power and, although the U-boats sank many ships, Britain was able to control the sea lanes during the First World War.

After the war, Winston spent a great deal of his time writing and painting, and he was outstandingly good at both. He was also becoming alarmed at the growing military might of Germany, led by Adolf

Hitler. Unfortunately, the British government would not listen to Winston's words of warning, and for the second time in just over twenty years Britain went to war with Germany.

In the next few months Germany attacked six countries in western Europe, and Hitler made it clear that Britain would be next, for he wanted nothing less than world domination. It was a time of great peril for our islands when Winston Churchill became prime minister. This is what he said on the day he became Britain's leader: 'I felt as if I were walking with destiny and that all my past life had been put a preparation for this hour and for this trial. I was sure I would not fail.'

And he did not fail. The Churchill spirit gave hope to the people of Britain. He often spoke to the people on the radio, and gave them stirring messages of hope. In one of his first broadcasts, he said, 'We have only one aim. Victory, victory at all costs. We shall go on to the end. We shall fight in France. We shall fight on the seas and on the oceans. We shall fight with growing confidence and strength in the air. We shall defend our island whatever the cost may be. We shall fight on the beaches; we shall fight on the landing grounds; we shall fight in the fields and in the streets. We shall fight in the hills. We shall *never* surrender.'

Now, in the summer of 1940 Britain, stood alone. Before Hitler could invade Britain, he had to defeat the Royal Air Force. So began one of the most decisive battles in history – the Battle of Britain. For weeks, hundreds of German bombers and fighters crossed the Channel to attack us and, although outnumbered, our fighter pilots in their Spitfires and Hurricanes went into battle. The skill and bravery of our pilots stopped the Germans, and in the middle of September Hitler had to abandon his plans to invade Britain.

When the Battle of Britain was over, Winston paid tribute to our gallant fighter pilots. He said, 'Never in the field of human conflict was so much owed by so many to so few.'

The war was to go on for another five years and, as Winston had predicted, it was long and bitter. He travelled to many parts of the world to meet and encourage the men and women in the armed forces. Wherever he went Winston became a symbol of freedom.

Victory over Germany came in May 1945. Winston spoke to the British people on Victory Day. 'This is your victory,' he said. 'It is a victory for the cause of freedom. In all our long history we have never seen a greater day than this.'

Winston Churchill died in 1965 at the grand old age of ninety. He is buried in a simple grave in the little village of Bladon, Oxfordshire, within sight of his birthplace. No man in history has had as many awards and honours conferred upon him.

He will be remembered as long as history is written as the champion of human liberty.

The Way You Look at Things

I belong to an organization which does small works of charity. One of its duties is to visit all the patients in the small local hospital. Every week two of us go round and have a short chat with each patient and give them a small bag of sweets. Most of the patients are very old and have been in hospital for years, and we get to know them quite well. Others are in for a few days while their families, who usually look after them, go on their holidays.

This particular day the weather had been very hot and close. A thunderstorm had broken in the afternoon and I had been caught in the rain and had got soaked. Naturally, I wasn't very pleased.

That evening, of course, the thunder and lightning and the heavy rain was what most of the patients talked about. Some had been a little frightened by the storm, some had quite enjoyed watching it and others had been asleep.

In one room two old ladies, sitting up in bed, described how the windows had been open and the rain had come in. One was rather distressed because it had rained on her bed clothes and the nurse had been slow in coming to her help. The other's face broke into a large, wide, beautiful

smile as she said, 'Yes, it rained on my face. It was the first time I'd felt rain on my face for eighteen years. It was lovely!'

It was then that I noticed that not only was she crippled with arthritis, she was also blind. Two people with two very different points of view. I think, perhaps the blind lady had the better way of 'looking' at things.

Captain Oates

Captain Oates was not an important man – in fact his only claim to fame is that he was chosen by Scott to join the ill-fated British expedition to the South Pole in 1910. It is in the manner of his death that he will best be remembered and revered.

Lawrence Oates was born on the 17th March 1880. He was educated at Eton College, and later entered the army as an officer. In time he rose to the rank of Captain.

In 1910, the year the expedition to the South Pole left these shores, there were only two natural obstacles waiting be overcome by man; one was to reach the earth's south geographic pole, and the other was the ascent of the summit of Mount Everest. The earth's North Pole had been reached in 1909 by the American, Commander Peary; and the Norwegian explorer, Roald Amundsen, had succeeded in discovering the north-west passage by sailing from the Atlantic Ocean to the Pacific through the Bering Straits. Amundsen was also keen to accept the south pole challenge.

So the race was on – Scott left McMurdo Sound on 1st November 1911, and Amundsen left the Bay of Whales shortly after – both heading south. Although Amundsen's overland route was some 96 kilometres shorter, the initial advantage was with Scott, for not only was his the easier route, but he also had the use of Sir Ernest Shackleton's charts, made only two years earlier. After ascending the Beardmore Glacier, and still some 275 kilometres from the pole, Scott sent the supporting party, men and dogs back to base. Now, on foot, he pressed on to the pole with only five men. Apart from Scott, these included Bowers, Petty-officer Evans (to distinguish him from the other Evans in the party), Oates and Wilson.

Scott and his men encountered some extremely hostile weather; terrible blizzards made them halt for days, huddled in their tent, not only for warmth but also for survival. It was after resuming their journey after one of these enforced halts that the men received a devastating shock – they saw unmistakable tracks of a sledge in the snow, and realized that the race had been lost. Crestfallen, the men pressed on, but a few days later their worst fears were confirmed when they came upon Amundsen's tent at the pole. It was surmounted by a Norwegian flag, which had been planted a month earlier. In bitter disappointment Scott's men raised their own cairn some distance away, and hoisted the Union Jack on top. This was on 16th December 1912; midsummer in the Antarctic. After spending three days carrying out scientific experiments, Scott and his men turned for home.

They realized that their return journey was not going to be easy; the weather might get worse (and so it proved), but the real enemy turned out to be a series of accidents. Evans twice fell into a crevasse causing him to have severe concussion, from which he died, and had to be buried. The weather worsened still further and two more of Scott's men became really ill. Wilson developed snow-blindness and had to be led, and Captain Oates' frostbite became so acute that he could scarcely put one foot in front of the other. Yet, in spite of these crippling handicaps, neither man uttered a word of complaint or criticism; they simply tried to hold on until their arrival at the next camp and the safety of all. But it was not to be.

On 17th March 1912, Lawrence Oates' thirty-second birthday, with a blizzard howling outside, he struggled to his feet and, rather than jeopardize the lives of his comrades, he raised the flap of the tent and said, 'I'm just going outside – I may be a little time.' He walked out and was never seen again. His colleagues knew he was walking to certain death, but knew equally it would have been useless to try and stop him.

Saint John must have had some similar sacrifice in mind when he said, 'Greater love hath no man that this, that a man lay down his life for his friends.'

Henry Parkes

Henry Parkes was born in Stoneleigh, Warwickshire, early in the nineteenth century and was soon left an orphan. At eight he was sent to work on a rope-walk, which is a long piece of ground used for twisting ropes, where the foreman beat him brutally and once knocked him down, where he lay unconscious for half an hour. As he grew older he worked in a brickfield and on the roads, breaking stones. Though he had never been to school he taught himself to read and write by pestering those who could. He read every book he could lay hands on and when he had saved a little money he walked to Birmingham where he begged an ivory carver to teach him his art. Within a few years he was a master-carver. Then, with a government bounty he sailed to Australia with a local girl he had married.

There was immense scope up-country, as there is today, for anyone willing to work long and hard. He washed sheep, rounded up cattle; did anything provided he was paid. He was never out of work.

When he had saved enough he went to Sydney, bought a lathe and set up as an ivory carver. He had the field to himself. All the time he read widely in his spare time and improved his education. Soon he was making a large income and looked round for channels of profitable invest-ment. He bought a newspaper called *The Empire.*

In 1854 Henry Parkes was elected to the Legislative Council; in 1886 he became Colonial Secretary; in 1872 he brought in the Public Schools Act and was elected Prime Minister of New South Wales. Five years later he was knighted, and was re-elected Prime Minister five times. He proposed that the various states should be united to create a Commonwealth and today he is known as Father of The Commonwealth. He had travelled a long way from breaking stones.

FABLES AND FOLK STORIES

The Fourth Wise Man

(Adapted from the book by Van Dyke)

Part 1

You will have heard of the Three Wise Men and how, led by a star, they travelled to Bethlehem to present their gifts to the infant king. But have you heard of the Fourth Wise Man, named Artaban? This is his story.

Artaban was a man skilled in the reading of the stars. When, one night, he saw that the planets Jupiter and Saturn were merging in the constellation of Pisces, the sign of the fish, which is the sign of the Hebrews, he took it to mean that a great and illustrious king was to be born among the Jews. He knew Caspar, Melchior and Balthazar, known to us as the Three Wise Men or magi, and agreed to join them in a journey to find and honour the baby.

In preparation he sold all he possessed, and bought three jewels, a ruby, a sapphire and a pearl, all intended as gifts for the king. These he placed safely in a pocket deep in his robe.

One night as he watched a perfect star grow large in the Western sky, he knew the time had come. He mounted his camel and headed towards the agreed meeting place with the other magi. His journey took him past the ruins of Babylon and through

grove after grove of palm trees on the border of the desert. He was, he thought, making good time when the moonlight picked up a figure lying across his path. He dismounted. It was a man, a Jew, seriously ill with marsh fever. Artaban was in a terrible dilemma. What should he do? A man was dying and he, a skilled physician, could perhaps save his life. But if he did it might be at the price of missing the other magi and having to face the desert alone. But to save this man was an act of love, and love is of God. He took out medicines from his baggage and began to treat the man. When the Jew began to revive he was astonished to find such a man tending him. 'I can give you nothing,' he explained, 'nothing for what you have

done for me – but you told me your quest and I think I can help you. According to our Scriptures the Jewish Messiah will be born in Bethlehem, Bethlehem of Judea. You should seek him there.'

It was gone midnight before Artaban reached the meeting place, the Temple of the Seven Spheres. There was no sign of his friends. On the topmost level he found a piece of parchment under a clay shard. It was a message. They had gone on. He was to follow them across the desert. Artaban was sad; he could not go on alone without camels and provisions. He must return to Babylon, sell his ruby, and buy all that was needed.

After weeks of travel, Artaban at last crossed the desert. He exchanged camels for horses and travelled now through fertile lands, through cornfields and orchards, and beside the lakes of the Jordan until, at last, he reached Bethlehem.

The place was strangely quiet. He thought perhaps the men had taken their sheep to the upper pastures. But in a low white house he could hear a woman singing as she hushed her baby to sleep. He knocked and entered. Then he asked if she knew of a most unusual birth in that town. She said that there had been a stir when three richly dressed magi had appeared a few days before asking for such a baby, but they had gone now. And the mother and baby they had visited, strangers to the town, had also gone.

Suddenly, as they talked, there was the sound of clashing swords, piercing screams, and women's voices crying that Herod's soldiers were killing their babies. The young woman went white and clutched her baby to herself. Artaban stood in the doorway, his rugged frame nearly filling it. A captain of the guard approached, demanding entrance. Artaban stood his ground, merely gazing into the man's eyes. His hand felt in his robe and then opened to reveal a glittering sapphire. The captain's eyes grew round with greed. He snatched the jewel, turned from the cottage and cried, 'March on. There is no child here.'

Artaban sank back, sad now that his second gift was gone. But the soft voice of the woman behind him said, 'God will bless you, for saving the life of my little one. May He be with you in your travels.' And Artaban felt again at peace.

Part 2

For thirty years Artaban wandered from country to country, always searching for the king. He did not find him, but he found many to help and blessing came to him in return.

As an old man he came to Jerusalem for a final time. In the streets were great crowds. That was not surprising, for it was Passover time. But there was also great excitement as if something was about to happen. Artaban asked one of a group where they were going. 'To Golgotha,' was the reply. 'There is to be a crucifixion. One Jesus of Nazareth is to be put to death because he said he was King of the Jews.'

The words struck a strange chord in Artaban. Could it be possible that *this* man was the one he had spent his life searching for? Might he be in time to offer his gift, perhaps even to save him? He followed the crowd.

A short way further on a troupe of Macedonian soldiers came marching down the street. The front two held a young girl. When she saw Artaban she pulled herself free and threw herself at his feet. 'Please save me,' she cried. 'I am of your country. My father was a businessman but he is in debt and I am to be sold as a slave to pay it back.'

Artaban looked at her with pity and compassion. He still had the pearl, the last of his gifts for the king. Should he use it to pay this girl's ransom or keep it in the hope that he might find him? Once more he avowed that the law of God is the law of love, and to save this girl would be an act of love. He produced the pearl and slowly placed it in her outstretched hands. 'Here is your ransom, daughter,' he said. 'It is the last of the treasures that I kept for the king.'

At that moment the sky darkened and a low rumble of thunder was heard. The earth heaved and horses and soldiers fell to the ground. Artaban crouched over the girl, protecting her. Several great shudders shook the city. The last dislodged a tile which fell, hitting the old man on the side of his forehead. The girl turned to look at him. His lips were moving, as if speaking to someone, but no sound could be heard. Then came a low but audible voice:

'Truly I say to you in as much as you have done it to one of the least of these my brothers you have done it to me.'

The old man's face filled with understanding and joy. His treasures were accepted. He had found the king.

Suho and the White Horse

Long ago, a poor shepherd boy named Suho lived with his grandmother in the ancient land called Mongolia.

Each day whilst herding their small flock of sheep on the grassy plains, Suho would sing aloud, his rich voice ringing out over the lonely hillside.

One night Suho did not return to his grandmother's home. His grandmother and the other shepherds were frantic with worry and were just about to organise a search party when they saw Suho approaching them carrying a small white object in his arms. It was a new-born foal.

Suho explained that he had found the foal abandoned on the hill top, very weak and helpless, and he was afraid for its safety with so many wolves roaming the countryside at night.

As the months and years went by, Suho cared devotedly for the foal who eventually grew up to be a splendid, spirited horse, much admired by the other shepherds.

One Spring, news arrived that the Governor was to hold a big race. As a prize, the winner could claim the Governor's daughter as his bride. The shepherds said to Suho, 'You have such a fine white horse! Why not enter the race?'

So Suho mounted his beloved white horse and rode off across the wide grasslands until he came to the field outside the town where the race was to be held.

Many fine horsemen took part in the race, which was long and arduous, but the white horse led the field, and, to the astonishment of all, won the race.

'The white horse has won! Go and summon the rider,' commanded the Governor. But on seeing Suho, the Governor was angry that he was only a poor shepherd boy. 'You shall not have my daughter. Instead take these three pieces of silver – leave the horse, and get out of my sight.'

Suho protested, but the guards beat him and banished him from the town.

It took a long time for Suho to recover from his wounds, and all the time he kept thinking of his beloved white horse.

Meanwhile, the Governor was well pleased with gaining the horse. He decided to throw a great banquet at which he would proudly ride the fine horse for all his visitors to see. But on the day the horse suddenly began to buck and rear, throwing the Governor to the ground, and galloped off into the night.

The Governor angrily shouted to his guards, 'Quick, go after the horse, and if you can't catch him, shoot him with your bows and arrows.' The white horse galloped with such speed that the guards could not catch him, but alas, many of the arrows reached their mark, and it was late in the evening that the horse, weary and hurt, was heard whinnying outside Suho's home.

Suho dashed out hopefully to see his beloved horse, but his pleasure was soon cut short when he saw how badly the horse had been hurt by the arrows. He nursed him night and day, but to no avail. The brave white horse died.

Shattered with sorrow, Suho lay sleepless for many nights, but when he finally slept he had a strange dream. The white horse appeared and said 'Do not mourn me any longer. Take my bones, hide and sinews and use them to make a musical instrument. If you do this, then I will be able to stay by your side for ever.'

Immediately Suho awoke he did exactly as the dream commanded, and made a beautiful instrument ornamented by the carved figure of a horse's head.

The instrument was so beautiful to hear and to play that other shepherds imitated Suho's fine work and made their own, and in the evenings the shepherds would gather and listen to the songs the horse's head fiddle sang. They forgot their weariness, and their hearts grew warm with peace and delight, giving them new strength for the days to come.

Among the people of Mongolia today, many play a beautiful instrument called a horse-head fiddle, which takes its name from the small figure of a horse's head carved at the top. If the head could talk, you now know the tale it would tell.

The Jealous Courtiers

There was once a very famous artist who lived in the little town of Düsseldorf in Germany. He did such fine work that the Elector, Prince Johann Wilhelm, ordered a statue of himself, on horseback, to be done in bronze. The artist was overjoyed at the commission and worked long hours at the statue.

At last the work was done and the artist had the great statue set up in the public square of Düsseldorf, ready for the opening view. The Elector came on the appointed day and with him came his favourite courtiers from the castle. Then the statue was unveiled. It was very beautiful – so beautiful that the prince exclaimed in surprise. He could not look enough, and presently he turned to the artist and shook hands with him, like an old friend. 'Herr Grupello,' he said, 'you are a great artist, and this statue will make your fame even greater than it is; the portrait of me is perfect!'

When the courtiers heard this, and saw the friendly hand-shake, their jealousy of the artist was beyond bounds. Their one thought was, how could they safely do something to humiliate him. They dared not pick flaws in the portrait of the prince, for he had declared it perfect. But at last one of them said, with an air of great frankness, 'Indeed, Herr Grupello, the portrait of his Royal Highness is perfect; but permit me to say that the statue of the horse is not quite so successful: the head is too large; it is out of proportion.'

'No,' said another, 'the horse is really not so successful; the turn of the neck, there, is awkward.'

'If you would change the right hind-foot, Herr Grupello' said a third, 'it would be an improvement.'

Still another found fault with the horse's tail.

The artist listened, quietly. When they had all finished, he turned to the prince and said, 'Your courtiers, prince, find a good many flaws in the statue of the horse; will you permit me to keep it a few days more, to do what I can with it?'

The Elector agreed, and the artist ordered a temporary screen to be built around the statue, so that his assistants could work undisturbed. For several days the sound of hammering came steadily from behind the enclosure. The courtiers, who took care to pass that way, often, were delighted. Each one said to himself, 'I must have been right, really; the artist himself sees that something was wrong; now I shall have credit for saving the prince's portrait by my artistic taste!'

Once more the artist summoned the prince and his courtiers, and once more the statue was unveiled. Again the Elector exclaimed at its beauty, and then he turned to his courtiers, one after another, to see what they had to say.

'Perfect!' said the first. 'Now that the horse's head is in proportion, there is not a flaw.'

'The change in the neck was just what was needed,' said the second; 'it is very graceful now.'

'The rear right foot is as it should be, now,' said a third, 'and it adds so much to the beauty of the whole!'

The fourth said that he considered the tail greatly improved.

'My courtiers are much pleased now,' said the prince to Herr Grupello; 'they think the statue much improved by the changes you have made.'

Herr Grupello smiled a little. 'I am glad they are pleased,' he said, 'but the fact is, I have changed nothing!'

'What do you mean?' said the prince in surprise. 'Have we not heard the sound of hammering every day? What were you hammering at then?'

'I was hammering at the reputation of your courtiers, who found fault simply because they were jealous,' said the artist. 'And I rather think that their reputation is pretty well hammered to pieces!'

It was, indeed. The Elector laughed heartily, but the courtiers slunk away, one after another, without a word.

The King and the Radishes

One day when King Louis the Eleventh was out hunting he became separated from the rest of the royal party. As he rode through the trees he came across a peasant's hut in a clearing. The peasant was gathering radishes from his garden, and the king, who was feeling hungry, dismounted and approached him.

'What is your name,' demanded the king, tapping the peasant on the shoulder with his riding whip.

'Pierre, My Lord,' replied the peasant, taking off his grimy hat and bowing low, causing the radishes in his hand to fall to the ground.

'I am hungry,' said the king, 'perhaps you would give me some of the radishes?'

'Gladly,' replied Pierre, 'but first allow me to wash them for you in the well.'

Pierre washed the radishes and handed them to the king, who sat on his horse munching away till nothing was left. By this time the royal party had found the king, and Pierre found himself surrounded by the king's guards.

'Stand clear,' cried the captain of the guards, 'don't you understand – you must not approach His Majesty the King of France!'

'Let him be,' said the king. 'He is a kind man, and his radishes are the best I've ever tasted.'

With that, the hunting party rode off and the peasant returned to his poor cottage with a marvellous story to tell his wife.

'The King,' she said, 'enjoyed your radishes, so why don't you take some to the palace. If he thinks they are the best . . .'

'No,' interrupted Pierre, 'it was just a whim. His Majesty must enjoy the finest food in the land – he won't want any more of my miserable radishes. He was hungry from hunting and anything would taste good in such circumstances.'

But Pierre's wife persisted, and so at last he gathered a bunch of big white radishes and made his way to the palace.

Pierre stood outside in the road until he heard the sound of trumpets, and soon the king rode out of the palace gates, closely guarded by his soldiers.

Pierre waved the bunch of radishes and the king, seeing him in the crowd, stopped his horse and called out to him:

'My friend the radish grower! I gave you no reward when last we met,' and, turning to the captain of the guards, he told him to lead Pierre into the palace. In the evening the king ordered a splendid dinner to be served, and he and Pierre sat down alone to enjoy it. The radishes were placed on a silver dish and the king ate them all except one – the biggest of the bunch.

When it was time for Pierre to return home the king gave him a thousand crowns, and to amuse him he placed the last radish in a jewel box saying:

'This will remind me of your kindness.'

All this happened when they were alone, and so as Pierre left the palace the captain of the guards asked him if he had been rewarded by the king.

'Yes,' said Pierre. 'For just a handful of radishes the king gave me – er – some gold coins,' anxious that the captain should not know how much he had received. Then he hurried on his way before any more questions could be asked.

The captain, who was very envious, thought about these words for several days and finally decided to present the king with a fine horse, thinking that his reward would be many times greater than the one which Pierre had received.

The king examined the horse and praised the captain for his generosity.

'I understand the reason why you have given me this splendid gift,' he said. 'I believe it is because you approved of my generosity to the poor peasant.'

When the court was assembled, the king sent for the jewel box.

'This cost me a thousand crowns,' he said, handing it to the captain, 'which I think is a fair exchange for your gift of a horse.'

The captain bowed to the king, and walking backwards left the court to examine his treasure, murmuring to himself, 'A thousand crowns, a thousand crowns.'

You can imagine his surprise when, on opening the box, he found only a withered radish!

The Three Rings

The Sultan of Babylon, wishing to test the wisdom of one of his advisers, asked him which of the three religions he considered to be the true one: the Jewish, the Christian or the Mohammedan?

The wise man, knowing that the Sultan was trying to trick him into giving a wrong answer, told the following story.

There was once a rich man who, amongst his treasures, had a ring of great value. He decided that the ring should always belong to the head of the family and so the ring was handed down to his son, who in turn left it to *his* son, until eventually it came down to a man who had three sons.

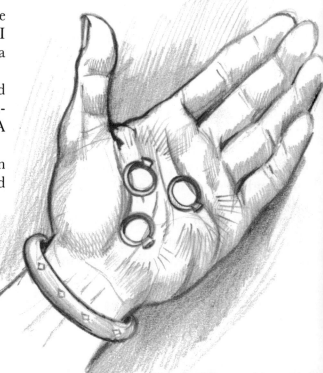

This man could not decide which of his three sons should succeed him as head of the family and so he had two more rings made secretly which were so like the first one that no one could tell the difference.

The young men, knowing that possession of the ring would give them great power, each in turn asked their father for the ring. The old man, who was equally fond of all three sons, gave a ring to each of them.

When the old man died, all three sons claimed that they were the rightful heirs, and went before the law courts each producing a ring in evidence. But the courts could not decide the question because all the rings appeared identical.

So it is with the three religions, the wise man told the Sultan. Each religion believes it is the true heir of God and obeys the commandments and has its own laws, but which is the true one is uncertain, as it was with the three rings.

The Brahmin, the Tiger, and the Jackal

Do you know what a Brahmin is? A Brahmin is a very good and gentle man who lives in India, and who treats all the beasts as if they were his brothers.

One day a Brahmin came upon a Tiger, shut up in a strong iron cage. The villagers had caught him and shut him up there for his wickedness.

'Oh, Brother Brahmin,' said the Tiger, 'please let me out. I am so thirsty, and there is no water here.'

'But Brother Tiger,' said the Brahmin, 'you know if I should let you out, you would spring on me and eat me up.'

'Never, Brother Brahmin!' said the Tiger.

So the Brahmin unlocked the door and let the Tiger out. The moment he was out he sprang on the Brahmin, and was about to eat him up.

'But, Brother Tiger,' said the Brahmin, 'you promised you would not. It is not fair or just that you should eat me, when I set you free.'

'It is perfectly right and just,' said the Tiger, 'and I shall eat you up.'

However, the Brahmin argued so hard

that at last the Tiger agreed to wait and ask the first three whom they should meet, whether it was fair for him to eat the Brahmin, and to abide by their decision.

The first thing they came to, to ask, was an old Banyan Tree, by the wayside.

'Brother Banyan,' said the Brahmin, eagerly, 'does it seem to you right or just that this Tiger should eat me, when I set him free from his cage?'

The Banyan Tree looked down at them and spoke in a tired voice. 'In the summer,' he said, 'when the sun is hot, men come and sit in the cool of my shade and refresh themselves with the fruit of my branches. But when evening falls, and they are rested, they break my twigs and scatter my leaves, and stone my boughs for more fruit. Men are an ungrateful race. Let the Tiger eat the Brahmin.'

The Tiger sprang to eat the Brahmin, but the Brahmin said, 'Wait, wait; we have asked only one. We have still two to ask.'

Presently they came to a place where an old Bullock was lying by the road. The Brahmin went up to him and said, 'Brother Bullock, does it seem to you a fair thing that this Tiger should eat me up, after I have just freed him from a cage?'

The Bullock looked up, and answered in a deep, grumbling voice, 'When I was young and strong my master used me hard, and I served him well. Now that I am old and weak and cannot work, he leaves me without food or water. Men are a thankless lot. Let the Tiger eat the Brahmin.'

The Tiger sprang, but the Brahmin spoke very quickly, 'Oh, but this is only the second, Brother Tiger; you promised to ask three.'

After a time, they met a little Jackal,

'Oh, Brother Jackal,' said the Brahmin, 'give us your opinion! Do you think it right or fair that this Tiger should eat me, when I set him free from a terrible cage?'

'Beg pardon?' said the little Jackal.

'I said,' said the Brahmin, raising his voice, 'do you think it is fair that the Tiger should eat me, when I set him free from his cage?'

'Cage?' said the little Jackal, vacantly.

'Yes, yes, his cage,' said the Brahmin. 'We want your opinion. Do you think –'

'Oh,' said the little Jackal, 'you want my opinion? Then may I beg you to speak a little more loudly?'

'Do you think,' said the Brahmin, 'it is right for this Tiger to eat me, when I set him free from his cage?'

'What cage?' said the little Jackal.

'Why, the cage he was in,' said the Brahmin.

'But I don't altogether understand,' said the little Jackal. 'You "set him free," you say?'

'Yes, yes, yes!' said the Brahmin.

'Oh, dear, dear!' interrupted the little Jackal, 'If you really want my opinion you must make the matter clear. What sort of cage was it?'

'Why, a big, ordinary cage, an iron cage,' said the Brahmin.

'That gives me no idea at all,' said the little Jackal. 'Show me the cage.'

So the Brahmin, the Tiger, and the little Jackal walked back together to the spot where the cage was.

'Now, let us understand the situation,'

said the little Jackal. 'Friend Brahmin, where were you?'

'I stood just here by the roadside,' said the Brahmin.

'Tiger, and where were you?' said the little Jackal.

'I stood here,' said the Tiger, leaping into the cage, 'with my head over my shoulder, so.'

But I still don't *quite* understand why did you not come out, by yourself?' said the Jackal.

'Can't you see that the door shut me in?' said the Tiger.

'How does it shut?, said the Jackal.

'It shuts like this,' said the Brahmin, pushing it to.

'Yes, but I don't see any lock,' said the little Jackal, 'does it lock on the outside?'

'It locks like this,' said the Brahmin. And he shut and bolted the door!

'Well, Brother Brahmin,' said the Jackal 'now that it is locked, I should advise you to let it stay locked! As for you, my friend,' he said to the Tiger, 'I think you will wait a good while before you'll find anyone to let you out again!' Then he made a very low bow to the Brahmin.

'Good-bye, Brother,' he said. 'Your way lies that way, and mine lies this; good-bye!'

Alibea the Shepherd Boy

There was once a bishop called Fenélon who lived in France in the seventeenth century. He had been appointed as a tutor to the King's grandson, and this is one of the stories he told his pupil to prepare him for the day when he would become King of France.

The Shah of Persia wanted to see how his people lived. He was tired of the flattery of the courtiers and so, one day, he set out alone to ride through the countryside. As he wandered amongst the hills he heard the sound of a flute and, looking up, he saw a young shepherd sitting on a stone. The boy was dressed in rags and his feet were bare.

The Shah spoke to the shepherd boy, whose name was Alibea, and was so impressed by his simplicity, his honesty and his good manners that he thought the boy must be the son of a nobleman in disguise.

'Oh, no,' said the boy, 'my parents live in the village over there. They are poor farmers, but we are very happy and I enjoy my work as a shepherd.'

It was a novelty for the Shah to hear such natural speech, and he wished that his son was as sensible as Alibea, so he invited the shepherd boy to the court.

Alibea did not want to leave the countryside, but he dared not refuse the Shah's invitation. At the court he was given handsome clothes to wear and was taught to read and write, and eventually he became the Shah's treasurer in charge of the crown jewels.

But Alibea was not really happy, because the courtiers were envious of him and he often longed to be home again on his hills with his sheep.

When the Shah died, and his son Sophi succeeded him, some of the courtiers accused Alibea of having stolen jewels from the old Shah, and advised Sophi to order Alibea to make a list of all the treasures.

Alibea did this and proved that nothing was missing. Then the envious courtiers told Sophi that Alibea had a secret chest which was always securely locked. Alibea said that the chest contained the things which were most precious to him. The new Shah ordered the chest to be opened, and there inside was Alibea's shepherd's crook, his old cloak and his flute!

Alibea told Sophi that he could take away all that his father, the old Shah, had so kindly given to him, but pleaded that the contents of the chest should remain there to remind him of his carefree days before he came to the court.

Sophi was impressed by Alibea's honesty and integrity, and appointed him as his chief minister. But every day Alibea went to the chest to put on his old cloak and to play his flute.

Town and Country Mice

A mouse who lived in the country invited a mouse from the city to visit him. When the City Mouse sat down to dinner he was surprised to find that his friend had only barley and grain to eat.

'Really,' he said, 'you do not live well at all. You must come to visit me and see how nice it is to live in the city and eat fine things.'

The little Country Mouse was glad to do this, and after a while he went to visit his friend.

The very first place that the City Mouse took the Country Mouse to see was the kitchen cupboard of the house where he lived. There, on the lowest shelf, behind some stone jars, stood a big paper bag of brown sugar. The City Mouse gnawed a hole in the bag and invited his friend to nibble for himself.

The two little mice nibbled and nibbled, and the Country Mouse thought he had never tasted anything so delicious in his life. He was just thinking how lucky the City Mouse was, when suddenly the door opened with a bang, and in came the cook to get some flour.

'Run!' whispered the City Mouse. And they ran as fast as they could to the little hole where they had come in. The little Country Mouse was shaking all over, but the City Mouse said, 'That is nothing; she will soon go away and then we can go back.'

When they did go back, the City Mouse had something new to show: he took the little Country Mouse into a corner on the top shelf, where a big jar of dried prunes stood open. After much tugging and pulling they got a large dried prune out of the jar and began to nibble at it. The little Country Mouse liked the taste so much that he could hardly nibble fast enough. But all at once, there came a scratching at the door and a sharp, loud *miaouw!*

'What's that?' said the Country Mouse. The City Mouse just whispered, ''Sh!' and ran as fast as he could to the hole. The Country Mouse ran after, you may be sure, as fast as *he* could. As soon as they were out of danger the City Mouse said, 'That was the old Cat; she is the best mouser in town, – if she once gets you, you're lost.'

'This is very terrible,' said the little Country Mouse; 'let's not go back to the cupboard again.'

'No,' said the City Mouse, 'I will take you to the cellar; there is something specially fine there.'

So the City Mouse took his little friend down the cellar stairs and into a big cupboard where there were many shelves. On the shelves were jars of butter, and cheeses in bags and out of bags. Overhead hung bunches of sausages, and there were spicy apples in barrels standing about. It smelt so good that it went to the little Country Mouse's head. He ran along the shelf and nibbled at a cheese here, and a bit of butter there, until he saw an especially rich, very delicious-smelling piece of cheese on a peculiar little stand in a corner. He was just on the point of putting his teeth into the cheese when the City Mouse saw him.

'Stop! stop!' cried the City Mouse. 'That is a trap! The minute you touch the cheese with your teeth something comes down on your head hard, and you're dead.'

The little Country Mouse looked at the trap, and he looked at the cheese, and he looked at the City Mouse. 'If you'll excuse me,' he said, 'I think I will go home. I'd rather have barley and grain to eat and eat it in peace and comfort, than have brown sugar and dried prunes and cheese, – and be frightened to death all the time!'

So the little Country Mouse went back to his home, and there he stayed all the rest of his life.

High But Empty

heads bend down, but the empty ones stand up erect.'

The nobleman merely blushed, and silently rode on.

There once lived in Paris a very proud nobleman who owned a beautiful chateau surrounded by lakes and woodlands and farmlands, and who employed many peasants to work on his lands.

The nobleman had a very high opinion of himself, and spent much of his time riding his horse around his estates making sure that everyone could see his fine clothes, his perfect and noble appearance, and view his superbly kept horse.

One day, the nobleman came upon a farmer trudging down the road. He was bent almost double from hard work and old age, and progressed slowly.

The nobleman asked the farmer, 'Why don't you stand up straight, and hold your head high as I do?'

The farmer did not reply immediately, but continued to walk slowly along the road with the nobleman riding behind him.

The nobleman was irritated that the farmer did not answer his question immediately, and he asked again, 'Why don't you stand up straight, and hold your head high as I do?'

At that moment, they were passing a field of wheat which was nearly ready to be harvested.

'My Lord,' said the farmer, 'do you see the field of wheat? The ripe and well-filled

The Jackals and the Lion

Once there was a great big jungle; and in the jungle there was a great big Lion; and the Lion was king of the jungle. Whenever he wanted anything to eat, all he had to do was to come up out of his cave in the stones and earth and *roar*. When he had roared a few times all the little people of the jungle were so frightened that they came out of their holes and hiding-places and ran, this way and that, to get away. Then, of course, the Lion could see where they were. And he pounced on them, killed them, and gobbled them up.

He did this so often that at last there was not a single animal left alive in the jungle except the Lion, and two little Jackals – a father Jackal and a mother Jackal.

They had run away so many times that they were quite thin and very tired, and they could not run so fast any more. And one day the Lion was so near that the mother Jackal grew frightened; she said, 'Oh, Father Jackal! I believe our time has come! the Lion will surely catch us this time!'

'Nonsense!' said the father Jackal. 'Come, we'll run on a bit!'

And they ran, very fast, and the Lion did not catch them that time.

But at last a day came when the Lion was nearer still and the mother Jackal was frightened almost to death.

'Oh, Father Jackal, Father Jackal!' she cried; 'I'm sure our time has come! The Lion's going to eat us this time!'

'Now, mother, don't you fret,' said the father Jackal; 'you do just as I tell you, and it will be all right.'

Then those cunning little Jackals ran up towards the Lion, as if they had meant to come all the time. When he saw them coming he stood up, and roared in a terrible voice,

'You miserable little wretches, come here and be eaten, at once! Why didn't you come before?'

The father Jackal bowed very low.

'Indeed, Father Lion,' he said, 'we meant to come before; we knew we ought to come before; and we wanted to come before; but every time we started to come, a dreadful great lion came out of the woods and roared at us, and frightened us so that we ran away.'

'What do you mean,' roared the Lion. 'There's no other lion in this jungle, and you know it!'

'Indeed, indeed, Father Lion,' said the little Jackal, 'I know that is what everybody thinks; but indeed there is another lion! And he is as much bigger than you as you are bigger than I! His face is much more terrible, and his roar far, far more dreadful. Oh, he is far more fearful than you!'

At that the Lion stood up and roared so that the jungle shook.

'Take me to this Lion,' he said; 'I'll eat him up and then I'll eat you up.'

The little Jackals danced on ahead, and the Lion stalked behind. They led him to a

place where there was a round, deep well of clear water. They went around on one side of it, and the Lion stalked up to the other.

'He lives down there, Father Lion!' said the little Jackal. 'He lives down there!'

The Lion came close and looked down into the water – and a lion's face looked back at him out of the water!

When he saw that, the Lion roared and shook his mane and showed his teeth. And the lion in the water shook his mane and showed his teeth. The Lion above shook his mane again and growled again, and made a terrible face. But the lion in the water made just as terrible a one, back. The Lion above couldn't stand that. He leaped down into the well after the other lion.

But, of course, there wasn't any other lion! It was only the reflection in the water!

So the poor old Lion floundered about and floundered about, and as he couldn't get up the steep sides of the well, he was at last drowned. And when he was drowned, the little Jackals danced round the well, and sang,

'The Lion is dead! The Lion is dead!'

'We have killed the great Lion who would have killed us!'

'The Lion is dead! The Lion is dead!'

The Twelfth Man

The men of Gotham loved to go fishing. One day, twelve of them set out to spend a long happy day with rod and line. When they reached the river they separated so as to leave each other a fair stretch of water. Some sat on the river bank, some stood in the water, and others leaned from the parapet of the little humpbacked bridge. The fish were biting well, and by the time the sun began to go down they had a really fine catch.

As they gathered their tackle together to set off for home, one of them said. 'Well, that's been a right good day, that has. What a good thing none of us fell in the river and got drowned!'

'Yes,' said another, 'we ought to be truly thankful. I suppose we are all here? We'd better count, just to make sure.'

So they began to count. Again and again they counted.

'How many do you make?' said one to another.

'I make eleven,' was the answer.

'Aye, and so do I,' said another.

So each of them asked all the rest but the answer was always the same. Every man counted eleven others, and forgot to count himself. Then they all became very worried and distressed.

'Neighbours,' said the spokesman. 'We have all counted us, and it is certain that where twelve set out, only eleven have gathered to go home again! One of our party is lost, maybe drowned! What shall we do?' They began to discuss plans for setting up a search, but they were in such sorrow for the missing fisherman that none could think clearly, or decide.

While they stood, trying to fix on a plan, along came a merry young fellow on horseback, ambling along and singing happily to himself as he rode. When he reached the bridge, he found it occupied by the men of Gotham, who by this time were all wringing their hands in grief at the loss of a dear friend and neighbour.

The cheery traveller stopped his horse.

'Well met, gentlemen,' he said. 'I can see that something is troubling you. Is there anything I can do to help?'

'Sir,' said the spokesman. 'We fear that one of our number is lost. Twelve of us came out fishing this morning, and we can count but eleven now.'

The stranger on the horse sat silently looking at them for a moment or two. Then he said, 'What will you give me if I find the missing man alive and well for you?'

'We will give you anything we have!' they all cried. 'Anything you ask for!'

'Will you give me your day's catch?' he asked.

'With all our hearts, and welcome!' cried the spokesman. 'It would be little enough to pay to have our brother restored whole to us! Do you agree friends?'

'Yes! yes!' they all said. 'Such help would indeed be cheap at the price.'

Then the fellow got off his horse, and asked them all to stand on the bridge, in a row with their backs to the parapet.

Tapping the first lightly on the chest, he said 'One!' and on to the next, 'Two' – and so on to the end. 'Eleven! Twelve!' he said. 'See, here is the twelfth man.'

Then the men of Gotham broke into happy cries of relief and gratitude.

'Sir', said the spokesman, 'We can find no words to thank you enough for finding our lost neighbour for us. Take all the catch with our thanks. We can now all go home as happy as we set out.'

So the cheerful rogue packed the fish in his panniers, and turned his horse towards the nearest market while the men of Gotham went back to their village rejoicing in their good luck in having met him just at the moment when they so much needed help.

Little Half-Chick

There was once a Spanish Hen, who hatched out some little chickens. She was much pleased with their looks as they came from the shell. One, two, three, came out plump and fluffy; but when the fourth shell broke, out came a little half-chick! It had only one leg and one wing and one eye!

The hen did not know what in the world to do with the peculiar little Half-Chick. She was afraid something would happen to it, and she tried hard to protect it and keep it from harm. But the little Half-Chick showed a most headstrong spirit. It would go wherever it wanted to; it walked with a funny hoppity-kick, hoppity-kick, and got along pretty fast.

One day the little Half-Chick said, 'Mother, I am off to Madrid, to see the King! Goodbye.'

The poor hen did everything she could think of to keep him from doing so foolish a thing, but the little Half-Chick just laughed at her. 'I'm for seeing the King,' he said; 'this life is too quiet for me.' And away he went, hoppity-kick, hoppity-kick, over the fields.

When he had gone some distance the little Half-Chick came to a small brook that was caught in the weeds and in much trouble.

'Little Half-Chick,' whispered the

Water, 'I am so choked with these weeds that I cannot move; please push the sticks and weeds away with your bill and help me.'

'The idea!' said the little Half-Chick. 'I cannot be bothered with you; I am off to Madrid, to see the King!' And in spite of the brook's begging, he went away, hoppity-kick, hoppity,kick.

A bit farther on, the Half-Chick came to a Fire, which was smothered in damp sticks and in great distress.

'Oh, little Half-Chick,' said the Fire, 'you are just in time to save me. I am almost dead for want of air. Fan me a little with your wing, I beg.'

'The idea!' said the little Half-Chick. 'I cannot be bothered with you; I am off to Madrid, to see the King!' And off he went.

When he had hoppity-kicked a good way, and was near Madrid, he came to a clump of bushes, where the Wind was caught fast.

'Little Half-Chick,' said the Wind, if you will brush aside these twigs and leaves, I can get my breath; help me, quickly!'

'Ho! the idea!' said the little Half-Chick. 'I have no time to bother with you. I am going to Madrid, to see the King.' And he went off, hoppity-kick, hoppity-kick, leaving the Wind to smother.

After a while he came to Madrid and to the palace of the King. He skipped past the sentry at the gate, and crossed the court. But as he was passing the windows of the kitchen the Cook looked out and saw him.

'The very thing for the King's dinner!' she said. And she seized the little Half-

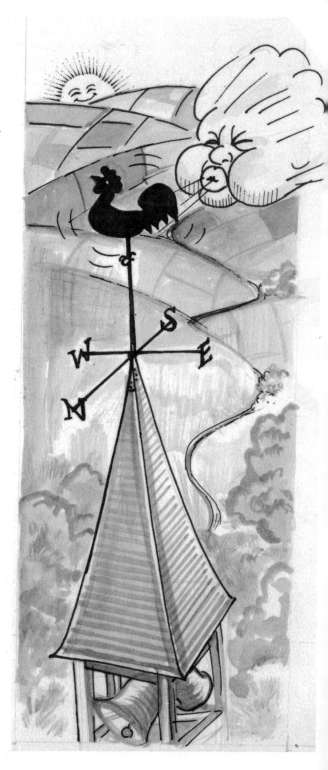

Chick by his one wing and threw him into a pan of water on the fire.

The Water came over the little Half-Chick's feathers, over his head, into his eyes. It was terribly uncomfortable. The little Half-Chick cried out:

'Water, don't drown me! Stay down, don't come so high!'

But the Water said, 'Little Half-Chick, when I was in trouble you would not help me,' and came higher than ever.

Now the Water grew warm, hot, hotter, frightfully hot, and the little Half-Chick cried out, 'Do not burn so hot, Fire! You are burning me to death! Stop!'

But the Fire said, 'Little Half-Chick, when I was in trouble you would not help me,' and burned hotter than ever.

Just as the little Half-Chick thought he must suffocate, the Cook took the cover off, to look at the dinner. 'Dear me,' she said, 'this chicken is no good; it is burned to a cinder.' And she picked the little Half-Chick up and threw him out of the window.

In the air he was caught by a breeze and taken up higher than the trees. Round and round he was twirled till he was so dizzy he thought he must perish. 'Don't blow me so, Wind,' he cried, 'let me down!'

'Little Half-Chick, said the Wind, 'when I was in trouble you would not help me!' And the Wind blew him straight up to the top of the church steeple, and stuck him there, fast!

There he stands to this day, with his one eye, his one wing, and his one leg. He cannot hoppity-kick any more, but he turns slowly round when the wind blows, and keeps his head toward it, to hear what it says.

The Elves and the Shoemaker

The poor shoemaker worked as hard as he could, but still he could not earn enough to keep himself and his wife. At last there came a day when he had nothing left but one piece of leather, big enough to make one pair of shoes. He cut out the shoes, ready to stitch, and left them on the bench; then he said his prayers and went to bed, trusting that he could finish the shoes on the next day and sell them.

Bright and early the next morning, he rose and went to his work bench. There lay a pair of shoes, beautifully made, and the leather was gone! There was no sign of anyone having been there. The shoemaker and his wife did not know what to make of

84

it. But the first customer who came was so pleased with the beautiful shoes that he bought them, and paid so much that the shoemaker was able to buy leather enough for two pairs.

Happily, he cut them out, and then, as it was late, he left the pieces on the bench, ready to sew in the morning. But when morning came, two pairs of shoes lay on the bench, most beautifully made, and again there was no sign of anyone who had been there.

That day a customer came and bought both pairs, and paid so much for them that the shoemaker bought leather for four pairs, with the money. Once more he cut out the shoes and left them on the bench. And in the morning all four pairs were made.

It went on like this until the shoemaker and his wife were prosperous people. But they could not be satisfied to have so much done for them and not know to whom they should be grateful. So one night, after the shoemaker had left the pieces of leather on the bench, he and his wife hid themselves behind a curtain, and left a light in the room.

Just as the clock struck twelve the door opened softly, and two tiny elves came dancing into the room, hopped on to the bench, and began to put the pieces together with their tiny little scissors, hammers and thread. No one ever worked so fast as they. In almost no time all the shoes were stitched and finished. Then the tiny elves took hold of each other's hands and danced round the shoes on the bench, till the shoemaker and his wife found it hard work not to laugh aloud. But as the clock struck two, the little creatures whisked away out of the window, and left the room all as it was before.

The shoemaker and his wife looked at each other, and said, 'How can we thank the little elves who have made us happy and prosperous?'

'I should like to make them some pretty clothes,' said the wife, 'as they are quite naked.'

'I will make the shoes if you will make the coats,' said her husband.

That very day they commenced their task. The wife cut out two tiny coats of green, and two waistcoats of yellow, two little pairs of white trousers, and two bright red caps, and her husband made two little pairs of shoes with long, pointed toes. They made the tiny clothes as dainty as could be, with neat little stitches and pretty buttons; and by Christmas time, they were finished.

On Christmas Eve, the shoemaker cleaned his bench and on it, instead of leather, he laid the two tiny sets of elves clothes. Then he and his wife hid away as before, to watch.

Promptly at midnight, the little naked elves came in. They hopped upon the bench; but when they saw the clothes there, they laughed and danced for joy. Each one caught up his little coat and things and began to put them on. They continued laughing and dancing until the clock struck two, then they danced right away, out of the window.

They never came back any more, but from that day on they gave the shoemaker and his wife good luck, so that they never needed any more help.

The Clever Magician

James was one of twelve servants in the king's service, and was especially proud that he was the king's favourite. It was he who stepped into the king's bedroom every morning, drew the heavy embroidered curtains and said, 'Good morning, your Majesty. It is eight o'clock and here is your morning pot of tea.'

Now each evening before retiring, the king would place all his beautiful jewellery on the large dressing table, but, without fail, would place his ring, which was his most treasured possession, on the bedside cabinet.

Towards the end of one particular winter, the king was taken ill and had to remain in bed for several days. Every servant in the palace made it his daily duty to visit the king in his bedroom and enquire about his health.

The morning dawned when the king felt much better. He was woken as usual by James and given his pot of tea, but when he got out of bed he noticed that his precious ring was missing. Now, all his servants had visited his bedroom during his illness, and he could just not imagine which one of them would have taken the ring.

That same afternoon, the king sent for his friend, the wise old magician, and told him what had happened. The wise old magician said to the king, 'Call all your servants to the great hall, and I shall speak to them.'

In no time at all, the twelve servants stood in a row before the king and the magician, and the latter said to the servants,

'You are all aware of what has happened, so I am here to try and solve the mystery for the king. I am giving each of you a stick of equal length. Put your stick under your pillow before you go to sleep tonight, and at nine o'clock tomorrow morning line up here as you are now and I will examine your sticks.'

The wise old magician then turned to the king, and whispered (but loudly enough for the servants to hear), 'One stick will be longer than the others by morning, and the owner will be the culprit."

The following morning, the servants lined up again before the king and the magician only to find that one servant's stick was *shorter* than all the others.

'This servant's stick is shorter than all the others,' said the wise old magician, 'because he cut a piece off it expecting that it would grow during the night. Your Majesty, there is your culprit.'

The Dagda's Harp

There is a legend that, a long time ago, there were two quite different kinds of people in Ireland. One set of people, the Fomorians, had long dark hair and dark eyes, and they carried long slender spears made of golden bronze when they fought. In contrast, the other race of people were golden-haired and blue-eyed, and carried short, blunt, heavy spears of dull metal.

The golden-haired people had a great chieftain who was also a kind of high priest, who was called the Dagda. And this Dagda had a wonderful magic harp. The harp was beautiful to look upon, mighty in size, made of rare wood, and ornamented with gold and jewels; and it had wonderful music in its strings, which only the Dagda could call out. When the men were going out to battle, the Dagda would set up his magic harp and sweep his hand across the strings, and a war song would ring out which would make every warrior buckle on his armour, brace his knees, and shout, 'Forth to the fight!' Then, when the men came back from the battle, weary and wounded, the Dagda would take his harp and strike a few chords, and as the music stole out upon the air, every man forgot his weariness and the smart of his wounds, and thought of the honour he had won, of the comrade who had died beside him, and of the safety of his wife and children.

There came a time when the Fomorians and the golden-haired men were at war; and, in the midst of a great battle, while the Dagda's hall was not so well guarded as usual, some of the chieftains of the Fomorians stole the great harp from the wall, where it hung, and fled away with it. Their wives and children and a few of their soldiers went with them, and they travelled fast and far through the night, until they were a long way from the battle-field. Then they thought they were safe, and they turned aside into a vacant castle, by the road, and sat down to a banquet, hanging the stolen harp on the wall.

However, the Dagda, with some of his warriors, had followed hard on their track. And while the Fomorians were in the midst of their banqueting, the door was suddenly burst open, and the Dagda stood there, with his men. Some of the Fomorians sprang to their feet, but before any of them could grasp a weapon, the Dagda called out to his harp on the wall, 'Come to me, O my harp!'

The great harp recognised its master's voice, and leaped from the wall. Whirling through the hall, sweeping aside and killing the men who got in its way, it sprang to its master's hand. And the Dagda took his harp and swept his hand across the strings in three great, solemn chords. The harp answered with the magic Music of Tears. As the wailing harmony smote upon the air, the women of the Fomorians bowed their heads and wept bitterly, the strong men turned their faces aside, and the little children sobbed.

Again the Dagda touched the strings, and this time the magic Music of Mirth leaped from the harp. And when they heard that Music of Mirth, the young warriors of the Fomorians began to laugh. They laughed till the cups fell from their grasp, and the spears dropped from their hands; they laughed until their limbs were helpless with excess of glee.

Once more the Dagda touched his harp, but very, very softly. And now a music stole forth as soft as dreams: it was the magic Music of Sleep. Slowly and gently, the Fomorian women bowed their heads in slumber; the little children crept to their mothers' laps; the old men nodded; and the young warriors drooped in their seats and closed their eyes: one after another all the Fomorians sank into sleep.

When they were all deep in slumber, the Dagda took his magic harp, and he and his golden-haired warriors stole softly away, and came in safety to their own homes again.

A Little Gossip for Little Gossips

Three young brothers, tired for the moment of toy cars and computer games, began to talk about their classmates. If any one of these had happened to be listening they would surely have agreed with the old proverb that 'listeners hear no good of themselves'.

Johnny Arnold was the first subject for these young fault-finders, but they did not linger long over him. 'A little baby' was felt to be a satisfactory statement of opinion about Johnny. Then came Kenny Williams, who was the biggest boy in the school. They all agreed he was a terrible bully. They then went through the whole class and at last came to Barry Grubb.

Barry was not too little to be ignored and not too great to be above criticism – and was one of their very best friends. He walked home from school with the boys, Adam, Nicky and Pete, every day of their lives – yet this is how they spoke of him.

'He's such a coward,' said Pete who, himself, ran behind a gate whenever he saw a dog. 'I hate a coward.'

'Yes,' agreed Nicky, 'and what a temper he has. He's always getting into a rage about something or other, and he sulks like anything.'

'Yes! Yes!' cried Adam, speaking very loud to get his turn, 'and as for greediness – well, I never saw his match. I think a greedy boy should be sent to Coventry.'

The mother of these three young gossips had come quietly into the room just after their discussion had begun, but they were so absorbed in their scandal that they had'nt noticed her. She put her arm round

Adam's shoulder, and the boys all looked up with a start.

'Stay where you are,' she said, 'and I'll tell you a fable. You won't find it in Aesop, but it ought to be put in the next edition.'

'A bull-terrier, a hare and a few other guests were asked one day to the house of Mr and Mrs Grunter, the pigs, to take a cup of tea, and to have a friendly gossip. They began by talking about the lion and finished up with the mouse, but nobody came out of the discussion very well.

The lion was considered to be loud and blustering; the fox was supposed superficial. The peacock was convicted of terrible taste in dress, but the one who they considered to be the worst of all was Charlie, the lap dog, who was considered to be very lazy and self-indulgent.'

'It's his cowardice that's the worst of all, though,' said the hare. 'Cowards ought to be swept off the face of the earth.'

'And then his temper,' put in the bull-terrier. 'He's that snappy you can't say anything to him. I just can't stand bad temper, snappiness and sulkiness.'

'What about the bull-terrier's own temper?' interrupted Nicky. 'I bet that wasn't much to go on about.'

'It certainly was not,' continued the boys' mother. 'The night before he had growled at his mistress who brought him his supper, and I believe he would have torn the paper-boy to pieces if his chain hadn't stopped Master Bully by being too short.' 'But let me carry on with the tale!

'Yes,' sighed Mr Grunter as he selected the biggest and most buttery piece of toast, 'his temper is terrible. However, we're all a bit hasty at times and he can be forgiven for that, but what I can't stand is his greediness. That's a horrible vice. I'll have another slice of toast, please.'

'He's a fine one to talk,' cried Adam. 'A pig is the greediest beast on earth.'

'Huh!' said Pete, putting his hands into his pockets. 'Those animals should have looked at themselves before running all the others down. Isn't there a proverb, Mother, about people who live in glass-houses not throwing stones?'

'Quite right, Pete. You have saved me from having to point out the moral of my story. Here are you three gossiping about your classmates, and you've only looked at the bad things. What about Johnny Arnold's kindness to animals, Kenny Williams' generosity, or Barry Grubb's perseverance at living with a handicap. And that's not the only thing. It's Pete who is most down on cowardice. Yes, Pete, I know all about the dogs. Yet cowardly Pete has no patience with Barry's timidity. You may well hang your head, young lad. It's Sulky Nicky who can't forgive Barry's little tantrums. It's Greedy Adam who eats up most of my mince-pies and who now wants to send his friend to Coventry because he gets less of Barry's sweets than he would like. I'm ashamed of you boys.'

'I hope you'll remember what I've said to you. Now come and give me a hug and we'll forget about the matter. Only don't pick holes in your friends another time. Whenever you're tempted to criticise anybody think about the fable of the hare, the bull-terrier and the pigs, and hold your tongues.'

Everything for the Best

In ancient days there was a rich and powerful king who ruled a kingdom that stretched from the Himalayas in the north to Sri Lanka in the south. Caravan-loads brought wealth into his capital daily, and his lands and fortunes were well governed by his ministers under the guidance of his uncle, Pratapsingh. This man's favourite saying was 'Everything for the best'. When challenged, he would reply, 'The troubles of this world, like sickness or famine, only enoble man's nature and teach him wisdom. So man goes on to perfection.'

One day the king and his uncle were out hunting. Some deer crossed their path. Pratapsingh wanted to return. He said the deer were an evil omen. The king, however, refused, and insisted that they hunted the deer. But the deer outran them, and the two horsemen found themselves lost and hungry. At last they found an apple. The king went to cut it, but the knife slipped and he cut his finger off. 'So! "Everything for the best is it?"' thundered the king, as he tried to stop the bleeding, and he ordered Pratapsingh to go. When he had gone, the king fell into a sleep.

Then, while he slept, he was discovered by Bhil tribesmen who were looking for a sacrificial victim for their tigress goddess. They were delighted to find such a handsome victim. They took him to a clearing, and tied him to a stake in front of an image of their goddess. Then they sang and danced wildly. After some hours they began final preparations for the sacrifice. They smeared the king with yellow and red powder. Suddenly, a cry went up. The king's missing finger was noticed! The Bhils fled in horror, for they had nearly presented an imperfect sacrifice to the goddess.

The king then realized that the loss of his finger had been for the best. But what of Pratapsingh who had got terribly scratched and bruised before he eventually got through the jungle to lead the king back to his capital. 'Yes,' said Pratapsingh, 'If I had not had such difficulty in getting through the jungle I may have come to your aid sooner, but I would have been overcome by the Bhils and made a substitute victim. Truly events have been true to my teaching: "Everything for the best".'

POEMS

Morning

by John Clare

The morning comes, the drops of dew
Hang on the grass and bushes too;
The sheep more eager bite the grass
Whose moisture gleams like drops of glass;
The heifer licks in grass and dew
That make her drink and fodder too.
The little bird his morn-song gives,
His breast wet with the dripping leaves,
Then stops abruptly just to fly
And catch the wakened butterfly,
That goes to sleep behind the flowers
Or backs of leaves from dews and showers.
The yellow-hammer, haply blest,

Sits by the dyke upon her nest;
The long grass hides her from the day,
The water keeps the boys away.
The morning sun is round and red
As crimson curtains round a bed,
The dewdrops hang on barley horns
As beads the necklace thread adorns,
The dewdrops hang wheat-ears upon
Like golden drops against the sun.
Hedge-sparrows in the bush cry 'tweet',
O'er nests larks winnow in the wheat,
Till the sun turns gold and gets more high,
And paths are clean and grass gets dry,
And longest shadows pass away.
And brightness is the blaze of day.

Diary of a Church Mouse

by John Betjeman

Here among long-discarded cassocks,
Damp stools, and half split-open hassocks,
Here where the Vicar never looks
I nibble through old service books.
Lean and alone I spend my days
Behind this Church of England baize.
I share my dark forgotten room
With two oil-lamps and half a broom.
The cleaner never bothers me,
So here I eat my frugal tea.
My bread is sawdust mixed with straw;
My jam is polish for the floor.

Christmas and Easter may be feasts
For congregations and for priests,
And so may Whitsun. All the same,
They do not fill my meagre frame.
For me the only feast at all
Is Autumn's Harvest Festival,
When I can satisfy my want
With ears of corn around the font.
I climb the eagle's brazen head
To burrow through a loaf of bread.
I scramble up the pulpit stair
And gnaw the marrows hanging there.

It is enjoyable to taste
These items ere they go to waste
But how annoying when one finds
That other mice with pagan minds
Come into church my food to share
Who have no proper business there.
Two field mice who have no desire
To be baptized, invade the choir.
A large and most unfriendly rat
Comes in to see what we are at.

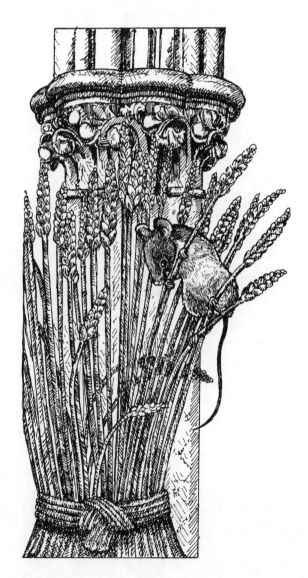

He says he thinks there is no God
And yet he comes . . . it's rather odd.
This year he stole a sheaf of wheat
(It screened our special preacher's seat),
And prosperous mice from fields away
Come in to hear the organ play,
And under cover of its notes
Eat through the altar's sheaf of oats.
A Low Church mouse who thinks that I
Am too Papistical and High,
Yet somehow doesn't think it wrong
To munch through Harvest Evensong,
While I, who starve the whole year
   through,
Must share my food with rodents who
Except at this time of the year
Not once inside the church appear.

Within the human world I know
Such goings-on could not be so,
For human beings only do
What their religion tells them to.
They read the Bible every day
And always, night and morning, pray,
And just like me, the good church mouse,
Worship each week in God's own house,

But all the same it's strange to me
How very full the church can be
With people I don't see at all
Except at Harvest Festival.

An Outstretched Hand

by Rod McKuen

Each of us was made by God
and some of us grew tall.
Others stood out in the wind
their branches bent and fell.
Those of us who walk in light
must help the ones in darkness up.
For that's what life is all about
and love is all there is to life.

Each of us was made by God
beautiful in his mind's eye.
Those of us that turned out sound
should look across our shoulders once
and help the weak ones to their feet.

It only takes an outstretched hand.

Roundabouts and Swings

by Patrick R. Chalmers

It was early last September nigh to Framlin' am-on-Sea,
An' 'twas Fair-day come tomorrow, an' the time was after tea,
An' I met a painted caravan adown a dusty lane,
A Pharaoh with his waggons comin' jolt an' creak an' strain;
A cheery cove an' sunburnt, bold o' eye and wrinkled up,
An' beside him on the splashboard sat a brindled terrier pup,
An' a lurcher wise as Solomon an' lean as fiddle-strings
Was joggin' in the dust along 'is round-abouts and swings.

'Goo'-day', said 'e; 'Goo'-day', said I; an 'ow d'you find things go,
An' what's the chance o' millions when you runs a travellin' show?'
'I find,' said 'e, 'things very much as 'ow I've always found,
For mostly they goes up and down, or else goes round and round'
Said 'e, 'The job's the very spit o' what it always were,
It's bread and bacon mostly when the dog don't catch a 'are;

But lookin' at it broad, an' while it ain't no merchant king's,
What's lost upon the roundabouts we pulls up on the swings!'

'Goo'luck', said 'e; 'Goo'luck', said I; 'you've put it past a doubt;
An' keep that lurcher on the road, the gamekeepers is about;'
'E thumped upon the footboard an' 'e lumbered on again
To meet a gold-dust sunset down the owl light in the lane;
An' the moon she climbed the 'azels while a nightjar seemed to spin
That Pharaoh's wisdom o'er again 'is sooth of lose and win;
For 'up an' down an round,' said 'e, 'gives all appointed things,
An' losses on the roundabouts means profits on the swings.'

95

The Glory of the Garden

by Rudyard Kipling

Our England is a garden that is full of
 stately views,
Of borders, beds and shrubberies and
 lawns and avenues,
With statues on the terraces and peacocks
 strutting by,
But the Glory of the Garden lies in more
 than meets the eye.

For where the old thick laurels grow, along
 the thin red wall,
You find the tool – and potting – sheds
 which are the heart of all;
The cold-frames and the hot-houses, the
 dungpits and the tanks,
The rollers, carts and drain-pipes, with
 the barrows and the planks.

And there you'll see the gardeners, the
 men and 'prentice boys
Told off to do as they are bid and do it
 without noise;
For, except when seeds are planted and we
 shout to scare the birds,
The glory of the garden it abideth not in
 words.

And some can pot begonias and some can
 bud a rose,
And some are hardly fit to trust with
 anything that grows;
But they can roll and trim the lawns and
 sift the sand and loam,
For the glory of the garden occupieth all
 who come.

Our England is a garden, and such
 gardens are not made
By singing:- 'Oh, how beautiful!', and
 sitting in the shade,
While better men than we go out and start
 their working lives
At grubbing weeds from gravel paths with
 broken dinner knives.

There's not a pair of legs so thin, there's
    not a head so thick,
There's not a hand so weak and white, nor
    yet a heart so sick,
But it can find some needful job that's
    crying to be done,
For the Glory of the garden Glorifieth
    everyone.

Then seek your job with thankfulness and
    work till further orders,
If it's only netting strawberries or killing
    slugs on borders;
And when your back stops aching and
    your hands begin to harden,
You will find yourself a partner in the
    Glory of the Garden.

Oh, Adam was a gardener, and God who
    made him sees
That half a proper gardener's work is done
    upon his knees,
So when your work is finished you can
    wash your hands and pray
For the Glory of the Garden, that it may
    not pass away!
And the Glory of the Garden it shall never
    pass away!

Escape at Bedtime

by R. L. Stevenson

The lights from the parlour and kitchen
    shine out
Through the blinds and the windows and
    bars;
And high overhead and all moving about,
There were thousands and millions of
    stars.

There ne'er were such thousands of leaves
    on a tree,
Nor of people in church or the park,
As the crowds of the stars that looked
    down upon me,
And that glittered and winked in the dark.

The Dog and the Plough and the Hunter,
    and all,
And the star of the Sailor, and Mars,
These shone in the sky, and the pail by the
    wall
Would be half full of water and stars.

They saw me at last, and they chased me
    with cries,
And they soon had me packed into bed;
But the glory kept shining and bright in
    my eyes,
And the stars going round in my head.

Desiderata

(Found in Old Saint Paul's Church, Baltimore, USA. Dated 1692)

Go placidly amid the noise and haste, and remember what peace there may be in silence. As far as possible without surrender be on good terms with all persons. Speak your truth quietly and clearly; and listen to others, even the dull and ignorant; they too have their story. Avoid loud and aggressive persons, they are vexations to the spirit. If you compare yourself with others, you may become vain and bitter; for always there will be greater and lesser persons than yourself. Enjoy your achievements as well as your plans. Keep interested in your own career, however humble; it is a real possession in the changing fortunes of time. Exercise caution in your business affairs; for the world is full of trickery. But let this not blind you to what virtue there is; many persons strive for high ideals; and everywhere life is full of heroism. Be yourself. Especially, do not feign affection. Neither be cynical about love; for in the face of all aridity and disenchantment it is perennial as the grass. Take kindly the counsel of the years, gracefully surrendering the things of youth. Nurture strength of spirit to shield you in sudden misfortune. But do not distress yourself with imaginings. Many fears are born of fatigue and loneliness. Beyond a wholesome discipline, be gentle with yourself. You are a child of the universe, no less than the trees and the stars; you have a right to be here. And whether or not it is clear to you, no doubt the universe is unfolding as it should. Therefore, be at peace with God, whatever you conceive Him to be, and whatever your labours and aspirations, in the noisy confusion of life keep peace with your soul. With all its sham, drudgery and broken dreams, it is still a beautiful world. Be cheerful. Strive to be happy.

Indian Prayer

(Traditional)

When I am dead
Cry for me a little
Think of me sometimes
But not too much.
Think of me now and again
As I was in life
At some moments it's pleasant to recall
But not for long.
Leave me in peace
And I shall leave you in peace
And while you live
Let your thoughts be with the living.

STORIES FROM SACRED BOOKS

Our Attitude to Holy Books

All the major world religions have holy books which are very precious to them because they are thought to be God's word to man. Believers therefore treat them with great respect. If you were a Sikh the book called the *Guru Granth Sahib* would be your holy book. You would keep it in a room by itself and every time you approached it you would bow.

If you were a Jew whose most sacred book is the *Torah*, or a Hindu whose most sacred book is the *Gita*, you would wash at least your face and your hands before touching it, and then you would keep your place and turn the pages with a stick. To handle it more than was necessary would be considered wrong.

Christians do not treat the Bible with such open respect, although believers honour it and keep it carefully. Surely none of us should ill-treat any of the books that other people regard as sacred? It is sad that some young people in this country have so little respect for the Bible that they may scribble in it, or tear it up and throw it about.

This is what a Russian bishop had to say about the Gospels which contain the stories about Jesus. He was talking to his churches 200 years ago, and nowadays we might use the example of a pop star as a person whose letter we might treasure.

'Happy are those who saw Christ in the flesh. But still more happy are we who see his image portrayed in the Gospels and hear His voice speaking from them.'

'If an earthly king wrote you a letter, would you not read it with joy? Certainly with great rejoicing and careful attention. The King of Heaven has sent a letter to you an earthly and mortal man, yet you almost despise such a gift, so priceless a treasure. Whenever you read the Gospel Christ himself is speaking to you. And, while you read, you are praying and talking with him.'

Whether or not you agree with what the bishop said, surely it is good to give your full attention to stories that have had an enormous influence on the people and nations of the world.

King David and the Prophet Nathan

In this Old Testament story there are two principal characters. The first is King David, the real maker of the Jewish nation. He had risen from being a simple shepherd boy to become the slayer of the giant Goliath, the follower and then the chief opponent of King Saul, and finally a powerful ruler successful in war and peace. He was respected by his subjects and feared by his enemies. He was, above all, deeply committed to his religion.

The second character is Nathan, the prophet. Prophets in biblical times were wise men renowned for their ability to look into the future and see how things would turn out. They were also men who did not think that power or personal possessions were of any great importance. They travelled widely throughout the country, usually taking their few possessions with them; they often dressed roughly, sometimes in the skins of animals, and were wild-looking.

King David must have been ill-at-ease when he saw the imposing, unkempt figure of Nathan coming towards him, for prophets always spoke their minds, even to kings, without fear or favour. Moreover, David had something on his conscience. Some little time earlier, he had wanted to make a certain young woman his wife, but unhappily for the king, she was already married to a soldier called Uriah, the Hittite.

In a moment of weakness King David had ordered that Uriah should be sent to war and placed where the danger was greatest. Before long he had been killed and David was now free to marry Uriah's widow.

Much to the king's surprise, Nathan did not storm into his presence and denounce him loudly. Instead he spoke softly and started telling David a story.

'There was a man in your kingdom,' he began, 'who was very rich, having many possessions including flocks of sheep, and herds of cattle, and goats. There was also another man who was poor and had only one small ewe-lamb which he loved and prized above everything else. Now the rich man envied the poor man for his one lamb so he killed the man and took the little ewe-lamb for himself . . . '

Nathan paused, and David sprang up in anger and shouted,

'What a despicable person you are telling me of, to be jealous of the poor man having just one lamb. It disgusts me that such a person should remain alive in my kingdom. Tell me his name and before God and by our laws, I will bring him to me to answer with his life for what he has done.'

There was a moment of silence, and perhaps during this time David began to see what lay behind Nathan's story. If so, he might just have been prepared for Nathan's quietly spoken words,

'That man is you.' (Or, as the first version of the English Bible puts it – 'And Nathan said unto David "Thou art the man."')

Of course David may only then have grasped the full meaning for, it is, of course, much easier to condemn others' failings than recognise our own.

How Moses was Saved

Thousands of years ago, there was a very wise and good Israelitish man who was a friend and adviser of the king of Egypt. Because of this friendship the king of Egypt had let numbers of the Israelites settle in his land. But after the king and his friend were dead, there was a new king, who hated the Israelites. When he saw how strong they were, and how many there were of them, he began to be afraid that some day they might number more than the Egyptians, and might take his land from him.

Then he and his rulers did a wicked thing. They made the Israelites slaves. And they gave them terrible tasks to do, without proper rest, or food, or clothes. They hoped that the hardship would kill off the Israelites.

But in spite of the work and suffering, the Israelites remained strong, and more and more boys grew up, to make the king afraid. Then he did the most wicked thing of all. He ordered his soldiers to kill every baby boy that should be born to the Israelites.

Very soon after this order, a baby boy was born in a certain Israelitish family. When his mother first looked at him her heart was nearly broken, for he was so sweet. But he was a boy! How could she save him from death?

102

Somehow, she kept him hidden for three whole months. But at the end of that time, she saw that it would not be possible to keep him safe any longer. She had been thinking about what she should do, and now she carried out her plan.

First, she took a basket made of bulrushes made water-tight with pitch, and then she laid the baby in it; then she carried it to the edge of the river and laid it in the flags by the river's brink. It did not show at all, unless one were quite near it. Then she kissed her little son and left him there. But his sister stood far off, not seeming to watch, but really watching carefully to see what would happen to the baby.

Soon there was the sound of talk and laughter, and a train of beautiful women came down to the water's edge. It was the king's daughter, come down to bathe in the river, with her maidens.

As the king's daughter came near to the water, she saw the strange little basket lying in the flags, and she sent her maid to bring it to her. And when she saw the child, so helpless and so beautiful, crying for his mother, the king's daughter pitied him and loved him. She knew the cruel order of her father, and she said at once, 'This is one of the Hebrews' children.'

At that moment the baby's sister came to the princess and said, 'Shall I go and find a nurse from the Hebrew women, so that she may nurse the child for thee?' Not a word did she say about whose child it was, but perhaps the princess guessed. At all events, she told the little girl to go.

So the girl went, and brought her mother!

Then the king's daughter said to the baby's mother, 'Take this child away and nurse it for me, and I will give thee wages.'

Can you think how happy the baby's mother was? For now the baby would be known only as the princess's adopted child, and would be safe.

And it was so. The mother kept him until he was old enough to be taken to the princess's palace. Then he was brought and given to the king's daughter, and he became her son. And she named him Moses.

But the strangest part of the whole story is, that when Moses grew up he became so strong and wise that it was he who, at last, saved his people from the king and rescued them from the Egyptians. The one child saved by the king's own daughter was the very one the king would most have wanted to kill, if he had known.

Kindness Repaid

The World in a Pillow

One of the most famous Christian saints of India used to spend much of his time alone, wandering in the high snow-covered mountains of his native land.

One day, when he was almost overcome with the cold, he caught up with a traveller who was finding it very difficult to walk through the thick snow. They walked on slowly together, helping each other as they walked. Presently, they came across another man lying exhausted in the snow.

'We must carry this poor creature,' said the saint.

'That is quite impossible,' said his companion, and he struggled on alone.

The saint bent down and picked up the poor man. After a great deal of effort the saint managed to lift him on to his back. The effort warmed him up considerably, and as he struggled to carry his burden he got warmer and warmer. In a short time the heat from his body warmed and revived the other man, and soon they were both walking through the snow helping each other. They walked together for some distance, and there was the saint's first companion lying dead in the snow.

'So it is,' said the Christian saint, 'he who would save his life shall lose it, but he who gives his life for another shall save it.'

(A story from the Chinese Tang Dynasty, adapted from the version told by Tao Tao Saunders)

Buddhism stresses that life on earth is exceedingly short compared with the slow changes of the universe. Wealth and poverty are seen as less important when we realise that the poorest beggar dies with no less than the richest king.

Long ago, there was a country inn at Handan in north-west China. One day a young man named Lu arrived there. He had just come from the fields and wore a short straight coat. At the inn he shared a table with an old man who had travelled a very long way, and after a while they began a conversation. They found that they shared so many thoughts and feelings that Lu began to feel that he had known the old man all his life.

Then Lu looked down at his shabby clothes and said, 'What sort of miserable life is this for a man?'

The old man looked at him in surprise, and said, 'I can see nothing wrong with you in either body or spirit. What is it that troubles you?' The young man sighed again and replied, 'With such a poor life as mine how can a man be happy?'

'If what you have is not enough, tell me what it is that would make you happy.'

Lu replied, 'I should like to be a person of importance, to be rich and honoured. I am already a grown man, and I have done nothing but work in the fields. Neither can I hope for anything more.'

As he spoke his eyes began to feel heavy, and a great tiredness came over him. The old man said, 'Come here on this couch. Use my pillow. It will make you rich and famous as you desire.' The pillow was made of green pottery and was unusual in those days in China, and there was a small hole at each end. He put his head on the pillow to sleep.

As he lay there, it seemed to him that the hole at one end of the pillow was growing bigger and bigger. It became so big that Lu was able to walk right into the pillow and back out the other end. When he did so, he found himself walking away from the inn on the road home.

A few months later, he married a beautiful girl from a rich family. Then he got a good job and was quickly promoted until he became a provincial governor. Further promotions followed until he had a senior post in the capital. At that time the Tibetans were invading the Chinese border and the General of the Chinese Army had been defeated and killed. Lu was given command of the army and he soon drove back the invaders and made the border safe. As a result, Lu received many honours, including a medal from the Emperor himself.

Within ten years Lu had risen to a very powerful position, and was one of the most influential men in the land. Such a position always invites criticism and Lu was falsely accused of having acted as a spy for foreigners. He was imprisoned on the orders of the Emperor. As they took him away he turned to his wife and said sadly, 'Once I was poor and safe. How I wish I had not been so ambitious!' He wept and took a knife to put an end to his life, but his wife stopped him. Later the Emperor released him but had him banished.

Some years passed, then evidence came to light that he was not guilty. He was released from exile and once more given responsibilities and honours. Lu became the head of a large and powerful family, with five sons who had married into noble families. He continued to live a life of luxury until old age and sickness, which even the Emperor's doctors could not cure, brought him within sight of death.

It was at this realisation that Lu woke. He saw that he was still lying on the couch at the wayside inn next to the old man who had lent him his pillow. The food they had ordered was just about to be served. Everything looked the same.

'Is it possible that I dreamed all that?' he asked the old man.

'The passing of a man's life is just like that,' said the old man. Lu was silent for a long time. Then, at last, he thanked the old man for allowing him to experience power and riches, poverty and degradation, life and death, and for fulfilling his desires. Then he bowed to the old man and left.

Jacob's Dream

Jacob was a runaway, an outcast. He had wronged his brother Esau, by robbing him of the right to inheritance of his father's lands, tents and flocks. Now Esau sought revenge, and Jacob was alone, far from home and afraid.

The thing that troubled him was something not at all easily obvious to us. At that time people believed that each tribe or people had a god of their own and that he cared for them in their territory and might well not have authority anywhere else. As darkness fell on the first night away from the safety of home, Jacob was scared most of all that he had left not only his father's tents but also his father's god behind.

The night was cold, and he had no shelter, no protection from wild animals. He wrapped a skin round him and lay down with a stone for his pillow.

He slept that night and dreamed a most meaningful dream. In his dream he saw a great ladder set up from where he was to heaven, and white glowing angels were going up and down on it. Above it God himself stood and spoke to Jacob, 'I am the Lord, the God of Abraham, your father and the god of Isaac. See, I am with you and will keep you.'

When Jacob woke from sleep the dream was still vivid in his mind and the meaning of it was clear. He had not left his god behind with his father's tents. God was also in this place, although he had not known it. At that realisation, Jacob was almost afraid. God was *there*, and he had not known it! Jacob whispered to God, '*This* is your house and the gateway to heaven!'

Early in the morning he rose and took the stone he had used for a pillow and set it up to mark the place. He called it Beth-el which means 'House of God'.

Zacchaeus, the Tax Collector

In the days of Jesus, Jericho was a very important and a very famous town. It lies in the Jordan valley at the head of the approach to Jerusalem, and at the crossings of the river East and West. Its climate then was hot and damp and vegetation was luxuriant. There was a great forest of palm trees, famous, sweet-smelling balsam groves and acres and acres of roses. Men called Jericho 'The City of Palms', a divine city.

The city was rich, of course, and its produce was traded far and near. This made it a fat land for tax collectors. Zacchaeus was a tax collector for the Romans, the chief tax collector in Jericho, a man most important but hated. All tax collectors for the Romans were hated by the Jews. They were regarded as traitors to their own people. Few made friends of them. The Jews would often have attacked and even killed them had it not been for their fear of their protectors, the Romans.

Since the tax collectors were already hated they seem to have had no qualms about making themselves even more objectionable. It was well known that all of them asked for far more than they were actually required to by the Romans, and lined their own pockets with the excess taxes they had taken. So they were rich; large houses, many servants, good food and luxury were theirs. *But* could these things ever be a compensation for being hated by all, and terribly lonely? Zacchaeus was aware that he felt a need for something. He hardly knew what exactly, but he needed some means of escape from the life he lived.

He had heard of Jesus. Had not all Palestine heard of Jesus? A good man, some said. A strange and wicked one, replied others. Why, he even mixed with low and evil people! Zacchaeus wondered if he would mix with him? He didn't dare to believe he actually might, but nonetheless he longed to see this man.

Jesus was coming to Jericho on his way to Jerusalem. On the day, almost the entire city crowded the narrow streets to try to get a glimpse of him. Zacchaeus too tried, but it was difficult. He was a very short man and needed to be at the front, but the crowd kept pushing him to the back. He must have *wanted* to see Jesus very much indeed. There was a tree nearby, a sycamore tree with wide lateral branches. Forgetting his pride completely, Zacchaeus shinned up it, high into the leafy branches where he felt sure he would be able to see without being seen.

A loud noise was coming from the direction of the city gate. A tall, dark, bearded man in white, smiled around him and uttered blessings as he made his way slowly down the street. He didn't look up. Yet below the sycamore tree he stopped and looked up into the face of Zacchaeus. A calm, clear voice called him by name,

Zacchaeus, his own name, and gave a welcome order, 'Hurry up and come down. I must be your guest today!'

Such a confusion of emotions beset the little man! The tone of voice this man had used was tender but insistent. He spoke as if he knew Zacchaeus already, had known and loved him for a long time. He actually *wanted* to come to his house, the house of a despised tax collector. No other Jew in the crowd would have done that. It was a beautiful feeling. He was accepted.

The people standing around were horrified. In their eyes Jesus had shown himself to be a bad man because he would befriend a tax collector. But Zacchaeus was touched deep in his inmost being. He did not need to be told what God required of him if he were to lead a new life from then on. He must give complete proof that he had changed from his greedy, selfish ways.

'Look, sir,' he said, 'I will give half my property to the poor and if I have swindled anybody I will repay him four times over.'

Jesus said to him, 'Salvation has come unto this house today!'

We are given no details of how Zacchaeus entertained Jesus in his house, but surely it must have been the happiest day of Zacchaeus's life.

A Story About Iona

Have you ever been on holiday in Scotland and visited a town called Oban? Oban is on the west coast; it has a very busy harbour with lots of fishing boats, and is also the base for the Caledonian ferries which sail to the many islands that lie off the west coast of Scotland. One of these islands is called Iona – it is very small, only about 3 kilometres wide, and just about as long.

Iona has some lovely sandy beaches, but it also has a large church and buildings rather like a monastery where a group of people live who are known as the Iona Community. As well as those who live there all the time, there are others who stay for shorter periods. Some of these people are pilgrims, and some are young people from the big cities on the mainland who have drug problems or perhaps have got into trouble with the law. Why is there a community like this on such a tiny island?

About 1300 years ago, one of the earliest Christian teachers and missionaries called Columba, or St Columba as he is now known, set up a monastery on this island. Together with a number of his followers they built a church where they worshipped God and prayed that more and more people would become Christians. Of course, it is not the same building that is used today, although you can still see what looks like a hole in the ground covered by a large stone which is known as St Columba's Cell. From Iona small groups of monks used to set out on missionary journeys to some of the other islands, and also to the mainland. Naturally, they had to travel by boats; these were quite small, and probably made of skin or hide specially treated to keep out sea water, and equipped with a small sail.

There is a story told that on one occasion two of Columba's monks set off on a long journey to some islands, and as their small boat disappeared over the horizon Columba called the remaining monks together and said to them, 'Our two brothers have gone on a dangerous journey, and will be away for many days. We must all pray that they return home safely when their task is finished.'

The monks said they would do this, but after a time they were so busy they often

forgot. Columba knew this, so one day he called them together again and told them that the two monks should have set out on their return voyage and would need the prayers of their friends as they crossed the dangerous seas where there were often very strong gales. Sure enough, one particular night a very strong gale blew up and Columba knew that the two monks would be in great danger, so he ordered the bell to be rung in the middle of the night calling his followers to come to the church to pray for their comrades. By the next morning, the wind had died down and as Columba looked out to sea he saw a little black speck far away. Gradually, this speck came nearer and nearer until they could see that it was the two monks safely returning.

When they landed, they said to Columba, 'We thought we should capsize last night, but then we remembered you were praying for us, and it seemed that we could hear the chapel bell ringing out over the stormy waves, and we knew then that we should be safe.'

Ever since the days of St Columba, Iona has always been a place from which missionaries have set out to tell the people of the Gospels, or Good News, of Jesus.

The Choice of Saul

Saul lived long ago in Palestine. The son of a farmer of the small tribe of Benjamin. Working in the fields he grew tall and strong but his family was of little importance and he imagined no great future for himself.

At that time the Israelite tribes were unsettled, aware that there had to be changes in their way of life. As a people, they regarded their God as their king. His representative on earth, the High Priest, Samuel, told them what they must do to please God. But there was a strong feeling amongst the people that things must change. Israel was surrounded by many strong enemies, some of them far better equipped for war than they were. The Israelite tribes argued that a strong, earthly king, such as other nations had was needed; a man who could command all the tribes. At last Samuel himself accepted this point of view and prepared to find out who would be God's choice of a king for Israel.

He gathered all twelve tribes of Israel together at a place called Mizpah. Then he sought to discover God's will by a very ancient method of selection. He drew lots, a process rather like throwing dice.

Faced by the twelve tribes of Israel he had a straw to represent each. He prayed that God would guide him and drew one.

It fell to the tribe of Benjamin, Saul's tribe. The new king would be of the tribe of Benjamin.

Then Samuel divided the tribe of Benjamin into families and again drew lots. It fell upon the family of the Matrites. Saul belonged to that family.

Finally, he took all the men of the Matrite family and drew lots to find the individual who should be king. The lot fell on Saul. All the people turned to look for him, to congratulate him, to honour him – but Saul was not there. Neither he nor any of his family had even considered the possibility that this young man might be the one chosen. During all the excitement Saul had been beyond the crowds, acting as a servant, looking after the baggage.

The people ran to call him. When he walked into their midst they saw him as if differently; tall and erect, strong and kingly. Here was the man they believed God himself had chosen to be their leader.

Life *is* an adventure. We do not know what opportunities may fall to us in the future. There could be something beyond the wildest dreams we have now. We don't know, but we can go on preparing ourselves conscientiously day by day for whatever life may bring.

Rebekah at the Well

Abraham turned to his son Isaac, whose name meant Laughter, and said 'In these strange lands where we are living now you cannot find a good wife. Far away in the land where I lived when I was a boy, perhaps there is a suitable maiden good and beautiful whom you could marry'.

So Abraham called his servant Eliezer, and said, 'I have work for you to do. Take the camels and go to that far land where I lived when I was a boy, and find a maiden good and beautiful to be the wife of my son Isaac.' Eliezer bowed low; it would be a long, long journey, but he was ready to go.

So Eliezer and several slaves loaded tents and food on to some camels, packed some presents of rich bracelets and rings to give to the maiden if they should find her; and started on their long journey. After many days they came within sight of the town where Abraham had lived years before.

Eliezer the servant was now worried. 'However can I choose the right maiden out of all those who live in this city?' he thought. Then as he drew near he saw that by the gate was the well where every evening the women would come with their water-jars.

The well put a thought into the mind of Eliezer; he halted, and made the tired camels kneel down to rest. Then he, too, knelt down and prayed to God.

'O God, help me to serve my master well,' he prayed. 'Help me to choose the right maiden for Isaac's wife.'

Then he thought, 'Isaac's wife must be kind, and a kind maiden is one who does kind things. I will wait by the well, and when the women come to draw, I will ask for a drink. If anyone gives me a drink quickly and gladly, I shall know she is kind; if she not only gives me a drink but offers to fetch water for my weary camels, then I shall know that she is the kindest and best of all, and that she is the maiden whom I seek.'

So Eliezer waited by the well, and presently, when the sky was pink with the sunset, the women came out of the city gate with their big water-jars. Among them was one maiden more beautiful than all, and Eliezer said to her, 'Pray let me drink a little water from your jar.' The maiden stopped at once.

'Drink, sir,' she said, and lowered the heavy jar and gave him a drink. 'Your camels look weary,' she said, 'and you have come from afar, perhaps. Let me fetch water for your camels too, till they have had enough.'

'Who are you, and where do you live?' asked Eliezer.

'My name is Rebekah, and my father is Bethuel, and my brother is Laban,' answered the maiden. 'Our house is near,

and we have plenty of food for you and for your camels, if you will come and stay with us.'

Eliezer thanked her for her kindness, and he gave her a gold ring and two gold bracelets from the treasure Abraham the chief had sent. For he knew that God had answered his prayer, and that this was the maiden, both good and beautiful, who should be the wife of Isaac.

When Rebekah reached home, Eliezer was made welcome by her family and told them of the true purpose of his mission and how God had guided him.

Then Eliezer took out the jewels of silver and gold, and the rich clothes, and gave them to Rebekah; and he thanked God who had helped him to find the right maiden, who was kind of deed as well as lovely of face. When the camels started back on the long return journey through the desert, Rebekah rode on one of them. And when Isaac saw how beautiful she was, and had heard Eliezer's story of her kindness, he loved her. He too was sure that here was a suitable wife.

The Shepherd's Song

David had many fierce battles to fight for King Saul against the enemies of Israel, and he won them all. Then, later, he had to fight against the king's own soldiers, to save himself, for King Saul grew wickedly jealous of David's fame as a soldier, and tried to kill him. Twice, when David had a chance to kill the king, he did not harm him; but even then, Saul continued trying to take his life, and David was kept away from his home as if he were an enemy.

But when King Saul died, the people chose David for their king, because there was no one so brave, so wise, or so faithful to God. King David lived a long time, and made his people famous for victory and happiness; he had many troubles and many wars, but he always trusted that God would help him, and he never deserted his own people, whatever happened.

After a battle, or when it was a holiday, or when he was very thankful for something, King David used to make songs, and sing them before the people. Some of these songs were so beautiful that they have never been forgotten. After all these hundreds and hundreds of years, we sing them still; we call them Psalms.

Often, after David had written a song, his chief musician would sing with him, as the people gathered to worship God. Sometimes the singers were divided into two great choruses, and went to the service in two processions. One chorus would sing a verse of David's song, and the other procession would answer with the next, and then both would sing together; it was very beautiful to hear. Even now, we sometimes do that with the songs of David in our churches.

One of his much-loved Psalms is a song that David made when he remembered the days before he came to Saul's camp. He recalled the days and nights he used to spend in the fields with the sheep, when he was just a shepherd-boy; and he thought to himself that God had taken care of him just as carefully as he himself used to care for the little lambs. The song goes as follows:

The Lord is my shepherd; I shall not want.
He maketh me to lie down in green pastures; he leadeth me beside the still waters.
He restoreth my soul; he leadeth me in the paths of righteousness for his name's sake.
Yea, though I walk through the valley of the shadow of death, I will fear no evil: for thou art with me; thy rod and thy staff they comfort me.
Thou preparest a table before me in the presence of mine enemies: thou anointest my head with oil; my cup runneth over.
Surely goodness and mercy shall follow me all the days of my life; and I will dwell in the house of the Lord for ever.

PRAYERS

This Universe

(Walter Rauschenbuch)

O God, we thank thee for this universe, our great home: for its vastness and its riches, and for the manifold life which teems upon it and of which we are part. We praise thee for the arching sky and the blessed winds, for the driving clouds and the constellations on high. We praise thee for the salt sea and the running water, for the everlasting hills, for the trees and for the grass under our feet. We thank thee for our senses by which we can see the splendour of the morning and hear the song of birds and enjoy the smells of the springtime. Grant us we pray thee, a heart wide open to all this joy and beauty and save our souls from being so steeped in care or so darkened by passion that we pass heedless and unseeing when even the thornbush by the wayside is aflame with the glory of God.
Amen.

A Russian Prayer for Animals

Hear our humble prayer, O God, for our friends the animals, especially for animals who are suffering; for all that are over-worked and underfed and cruelly treated; for all wistful creatures in captivity that beat against their bars; for any that are hunted or lost or deserted or frightened or hungry; for all that are in pain or dying; for all that must be put to death. We entreat for them all thy mercy and pity; and for those who deal with them we ask a heart of compassion and gentle hands and kindly words. Make us ourselves to be true friend to animals and so to share the blessing of the merciful.
Amen.

The Dog's Prayer

O Lord of all creatures, make the man, my master, as faithful to other men as I am to him. Make him as loving to his family and friends as I am to him. Make him the honest guardian of the blessings which you have entrusted to him as I honestly guard his own.

Give him, O Lord, an easy and spontaneous smile, easy and spontaneous as when I wag my tail. May he be as readily grateful as I am quick to lick his hand. Grant him patience equal to mine, when I wait his return without complaining. Give him my courage, my readiness to sacrifice everything in all circumstances, even life itself. Keep for him the youthfulness of my heart and the cheerfulness of my thoughts. O Lord of all creatures, as I am always truly a dog, grant that he may be always truly a man.
Amen.

Learning Religion at School

We learn religion all day long.

We learn it in arithmetic by accuracy.

We learn it in language by learning to say what we mean – yea, yea, or nay, nay.

We learn it in history by humanity.

We learn it in geography by breadth of mind.

We learn it in handicraft by thoroughness.

We learn it in astronomy by reverence.

We learn it by good manners to one another and by truthfulness in all things.

We learn as students to build the Church of Christ out of the actual relationships in which we stand to our teachers and to our schoolfellows.

Amen

Prayer

(by Rita Snowden)

O God it is easy to love the whole world but hard to love the person one works next to;

O God it is easy to campaign for world peace, but hard to contribute to the peace within my own home;

O God it is easy to be fascinated with some new truth and miss you in the things I have known so long;

O God it is easy to share my home and possessions with people I like

Teach me how to be generous towards thee.

Enable me today to say something that will make a difference to the discouraged

to the inexperienced

to the despairing

Let no selfish concern with my own affairs shut me off from any today. For your love's sake.

Amen.

The Most Important Words

From Tomorrow

(A Prayer from a Child in a Nazi Death Camp)

The six most important words in the world:
I ADMIT I MADE A MISTAKE
The five most important words in the world:
YOU DID A GOOD JOB
The four most important words in the world:
WHAT IS YOUR OPINION?
The three most important words in the world:
IF YOU PLEASE
The two most important words in the world:
THANK YOU
The most important word in the world:
WE
The least important word in the world:
I

From tomorrow on I shall be sad.
From tomorrow on.
Not today. Today I will be glad.
And every day no matter how bitter it may
    be,
I shall say:
From tomorrow on I shall be sad.
Not today.

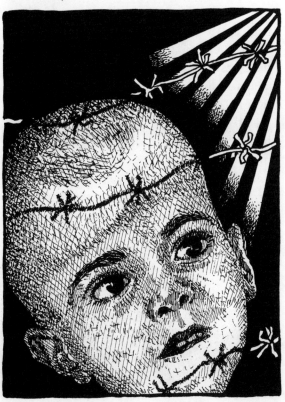

Gonnal Singh's Prayer

(A Seventeenth Century Sikh)

Lord, thou art the Hindu, the Muslim, the
   Turk and the Feringhee; thou art the
   Persian, the Sanskritian, the Arabian;
Thou art the speech . . . thou art the war-
   rior clad in shining armour and thou art
   the peace supreme.
Thou art man, woman, child and God!
Thou art the flute players, the herdsman
   that goes grazing his dumb cows!
Thou bestoweth love and thou givest thy-
   self to all!
Thou art the protector of life and the giver
   of all prosperity!
Thou art the cure of all sorrow and suffer-
   ing.
In all shapes and everywhere that art dear
   to me, in every form thou art thyself.
Thou art my now – my beginning and my
   end.

Days

(by John Gowan)

I wasted it
It's gone
And I repent
The precious day
You gave me
Came and went!
It wasn't really mine
To throw away.
I'm sorry that I
Used it up that way.
Remind me that my days are just on loan.
Forgive me
When I treat them
As my own.
But here's another,
Fresh and clean
And new.
Help me to use it
Wisely Lord
For You.

The Zend Avesta

(Zoroastrian)

All that we ought to have thought and
  have not thought;
All that we ought to have said and have
  not said.
All that we ought to have done and have
  not done,
All that we ought not to have thought and
  yet have thought;
All that we ought not to have spoken and
  yet have spoken
All that we ought not to have done and yet
  have done
For thoughts, words, and works, pray I
  O God for forgiveness
And repent with penance.

Conformity

(by John Gowan)

I hate to be less
Than popular
I like to be liked
That's bad?
And sometimes
It keeps me silent
When I should speak out
That's sad.
Forgive me
When I've said nothing
Just to stay one of the gang
Betrayed what I most
Believe in
And let the truth go hang!

I want to speak out
When I should, Lord
So give me the nerve I need
And if I must suffer for it
You'll grant me the grace
Agreed?

The Media

We pray that we don't take as gospel all that we read in newspapers,

We pray that we think for ourselves without being unduly influenced by television,

We pray that we don't imitate violence, injustice and hatred,

We pray that we may acquire knowledge so that we have the ability to make up our own mind.

Early Prayer

Jesus, Saviour, friend of children,
Be a friend to me;
Take my hand, and ever keep me
Close to thee.

Teach me how to grow in goodness,
Daily as I grow;
Thous hast been a child, and surely
Thou dost know.

Step by step, oh! lead me onward,
Upward into youth:
Wiser, stronger, still becoming
In thy truth.

Never leave me, nor forsake me,
Ever be my friend;
For I need thee from life's dawning
To its end.

An Irish Blessing

May the road rise to meet you.
May the wind be always at your back.
May the sun shine warm upon your face.
The rains fall soft upon your fields and,
    until we meet again,
May God hold you in the palm of his
    hand.

FICTION

The Larks in the Cornfield

There was once a family of Larks who lived with their mother in a nest in a cornfield. When the corn was ripe the mother Lark watched very carefully to see if there were any sign of the reapers' coming, for she knew that when they came their sharp knives would cut down the nest and hurt the baby Larks. So everyday, when she went out for food, she told the little Larks to look and listen very closely to everything that went on, and to tell her all they saw and heard when she came home.

One day when she came home the little Larks were much frightened.

'Oh, Mother!' they said, 'you must move us away tonight! The farmer was in the field today, and he said, "The corn is ready to cut; we must call in the neighbours to help." And then he told his son to go out tonight and ask all the neighbours to come and reap the corn tomorrow.'

The mother Lark laughed. 'Don't be frightened,' she said; 'if he waits for his neighbours to reap the corn we shall have plenty of time to move; tell me what he says tomorrow.'

The next night the little Larks were quite trembling with fear; the moment their mother got home they cried out, 'Mother, you must surely move us tonight! The farmer came today and said, "The corn is getting too ripe; we cannot wait for our neighbours; we must ask our relatives to help us." And then he called his son and told him to ask all the uncles and cousins to come tomorrow and cut the corn. Shall we not move tonight?'

'Don't worry,' said the Mother Lark; 'the uncles and cousins have plenty of reaping to do for themselves; we'll not move yet.'

The third night, when the mother Lark came home, the baby Larks said, 'Mother, the farmer came to the field today, and when he looked at the corn he was quite angry; he said, "This will never do! The corn is getting too ripe; it's no use to wait for our relatives, we shall have to cut this corn ourselves." And then he called his son and said, "Go out tonight and hire reapers, and tomorrow we will begin to cut."'

'Well,' said the mother, 'that is another story; when a man begins to do his own business, instead of asking somebody else to do it, things get done. I will move you out tonight.'

The Fir Tree

Once there was a Little Fir Tree which stood in the middle of the great forest. The Little Fir Tree was very unhappy because he was not big like the other trees. When the birds came flying into the woods and lit on the branches of the big trees and built their nests there, he used to call up to them.

'Come down, come down, and rest in my branches!' But they always said,

'Oh, no, you are too little!'

In the winter the white snow fell softly, and covered the great trees all over with wonderful caps and coats of white. The Little Fir Tree would call up,

'Oh, please, dear snow, give me a cap too! I want to play, too!' But the snow always said,

'Oh no, you are too little, you are too little!'

The worst of all was when men came into the wood to cut the big trees down and carry them away. The Little Fir Tree listened to the others talking, and heard them say that when you were carried away, you might become the mast of a mighty ship, and go far away over the ocean; or you might be part of a fine house in a great city, and see much of life. But the Little Fir Tree was always too small; the men passed him by.

However, one cold winter's morning, the men came to the area near the Little Fir Tree, and looked all about.

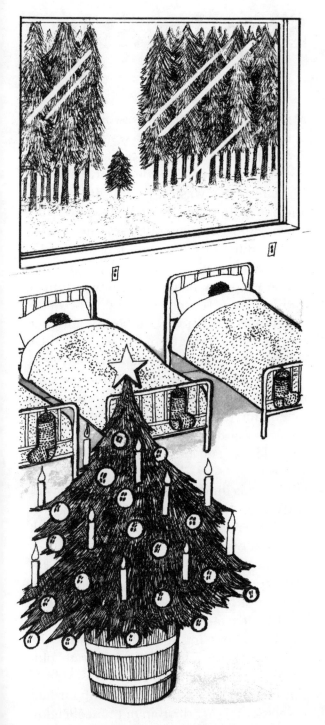

'There are none little enough,' they said.

But here is one,' said one of the men, 'it is just little enough.' And he touched the Little Fir Tree.

The Little Fir Tree was so happy, because he knew they were about to cut him down. And when he was being carried away on the sledge he lay wondering, whether he would be the mast of a ship or part of a fine city house. But when they came to the town he was taken out and set upright in a tub in a row of other fir trees, all small, but none so little as he.

People kept coming to look at the trees and to take them away. But always when they saw the Little Fir Tree they shook their heads and said,

'It's too little, too little.'

Until, finally, two children came along. When they saw the Little Fir Tree they cried out,

'We'll take this one; it is just little enough!'

They carried him away, between them. And the happy Little Fir Tree spent all his time wondering what it could be that he was just little enough for. He kept wondering, while they took him in through some big doors, and set him up on the table, in a bare little room. Very soon they went away, and came back with a big basket. They then took things out of the basket and began to play with the Little Fir Tree, just as he had often begged the snow and the birds to do. When he looked down at himself, he saw that he was all hung with gold and silver chains! There were pink and white candles in his arms and strings of white fluffy stuff drooping around him. His twigs held little gold and silver stars, but best of all was the beautiful gold star on his head. The Little Fir Tree could not breathe, for joy and wonder. What was it that he was, now? Why was this glory for him?

After a time everyone went away and left him. It grew dusk, and the Little Fir Tree began to hear strange sounds through the closed doors. He was beginning to be lonely. It grew more and more shadowy.

All at once, the doors opened and the two children came in. Two ladies were with them. They came up to the Little Fir Tree and quickly lit all the pink and white candles. Then the two ladies took hold of the table with the Little Fir Tree on it and pushed it, very smoothly and quickly, out of the doors, across a hall, and in at another door.

The Little Fir Tree had a sudden sight of a long room with many small white beds in it, of children propped up on pillows in the beds, and of other children in great wheeled chairs. He wondered why all the children looked so white and tired; he did not know that he was in a hospital. But before he could wonder any more his breath was quite taken away by the shouts of joy the children gave.

Step by Step

Mrs Hobson sat at her sewing machine and stared at the pile of work. She had decided to make clothes for all her children for Christmas in order to save money. But Christmas was only eight days away, and she hadn't done a stitch. Two dressing gowns, a sweater, two blouses and a skirt had been her original plan, but she hadn't even started yet.

She felt a mixture of tiredness, sadness and lethargy. It seemed ironic to be making things for those she loved and yet hating every minute of it. Yet she just couldn't find the energy to start sewing.

As she sat there gazing out into the cold deserted street she saw Mr Andrews, their neighbour from next door. He had had a stroke recently and could now only walk very slowly, and he was very unsteady on his feet.

Since his illness he had to relearn how to walk and had to practise every day to build up his strength and courage. It took every bit of concentration he could muster to command his legs and arms to coordinate his slow trek to the end of the street and back.

Mrs Hobson watched his slow progress, each step carrying him only a few centimetres at a time. Then her blood ran cold. Right in front of Mr Andrews was a dustbin surrounded by litter. A neighbour had carelessly left her dustbin out for collection right in the middle of the pavement. To get by, Mr Andrews would have to step off the kerb or balance himself on the slight incline of a driveway.

She watched him pause and study the problem. Should she run out and help him – but wait – he had already started his detour alone and if she surprised him suddenly he might fall.

Once he tottered and almost fell, but instead of wasting breath calling out, he steadied himself and slowly, very, very slowly he manoeuvred around the obstacles, back onto the pavement with ponderous determination and patience, and continued his walk.

Mrs Hobson examined the pile of materials and patterns in front of her and suddenly felt embarrassed. Here she sat with all her faculties intact except one – the will to begin, to take the first step. And there was Mr Andrews!

She realised that her sewing machine, the same as Mr Andrews' faltering legs, contained no magic. Work was required and she realised that you can't get anywhere if you can't start. Soon Mrs Hobson's machine was whirring away and steadily the clothes started to take shape.

She enjoyed the days up to Christmas with her new-found lease of life, and she remembered for a long time the thought that Mr Andrews had unknowingly instilled: 'You can only go anywhere one step at a time.'

Don't Look at the Clock

The two young men hesitated outside the huge office block, and each taking a deep breath, hurried inside. Up in the lift to the twenty-third floor they went, to start their careers with the Bank.

'Tony Palmer,' said the tall, fair boy extending his hand to the other, dark-haired young man. 'It's my first day here, is it yours, too?'

'Yes,' replied the other, 'I'm Paul Newton, and it's my first day as well. I'm really looking forward to working instead of going to College.'

'Oh, well', said Tony, 'it'll pass the time, I suppose, and we get paid for it as well.'

As time went by, Tony was seen to be the one who arrived exactly on time, never a minute before and never a minute late, and who put his work aside immediately the clock said lunchtime or time to go home in the evening. It was also noted that he never did more than his share, never offered to help anyone over-burdened with work, but he was considered to be charming, good mannered and always well-dressed.

Paul, on the other hand, was a very hard worker, always cheerful and willing to help anyone. He too arrived on time in the mornings, but always keen to finish whatever task he was engaged in, whatever time the clock said, lunchtime or end of the day.

As the two young men matured, they became very good friends, but Tony was always gently jibing at Paul for his dedication to his work. 'It won't get you anywhere,' he said. 'We started out together, and despite our different approaches to the

job, we're still on a par, even with your doing all that extra work, and putting in extra time. Personally, I'm only staying there out of security. If I thought I could get a better job with more money for doing less, I'd go and get it.'

One day a notice went up in the office. A Senior Manager was about to retire, and staff were asked to apply for his position. 'I'm going to try for that,' Tony told Paul. 'I'm sure I stand a chance as the Managing Director of that division has noticed me', and he preened himself a little.

'Yes,' replied Paul. 'I'm going to apply too.'

'Oh, I don't think they'll let you move,' said Tony. 'I think they think you're too valuable where you are. After all, you are now a Head of Section and you know everything there is to know about your particular department. I know your Director thinks a lot of you.'

'Oh, do you really think so?' asked Paul. 'Well, I'll give it a try, anyway. The experience of a tough interview at that level will be good for me, if I get that far.' And so they parted, Tony to go to the hairdresser, and Paul to sort out a problem in his section.

When the results of the applications and interviews were posted on the noticeboard, everyone was amazed. Paul had got the job as Senior Manager. Everyone was delighted for him, even Tony, who felt a bit disgruntled because he felt that he was right for promotion himself as he had been at the Bank the same length of time as Paul. Tony decided to go to his own Head of Section to talk with him about the prospects for promotion.

'Well, Tony,' the Manager explained, 'Paul was offered the position because he was prepared to work extra hard, and to help other people with their work problems, and also because he never looked at the clock but carried on working until he had finished, no matter what the time, before he broke for lunch or to go home in the evening. You'd do well to take a leaf out of his book. Being charming and well-dressed won't get you to the top, but hard work will.'

The Gulls of Salt Lake

Many years ago, pioneers from the Atlantic coast crossed the Mississippi River and journeyed through the plains of Central North America. Further west, still, they came across the great Rocky Mountains, and, in the very midst of the mountains, a valley of brown, bare, desert soil. Although the valley itself received very little rain, the snow on the mountain-tops sent down little streams of pure water, the winds were gentle, and lying like a blue jewel at the foot of the hills was a marvellous lake of salt water, an inland sea. So the pioneers settled there and built themselves huts and cabins for the first winter.

By the following spring, the provisions they had brought in their wagons were nearly gone. All their lives now depended on the crops which they could raise in the valley. They had made the barren land fertile by spreading water from the little streams over it, what we call 'irrigating', and they planted enough grain and vegetables for all the people. Everyone helped, and everyone watched for the sprouting, with hopes and prayers.

In good time the seeds sprouted, and the dry, brown earth was covered with a carpet of tender, green, growing things. And from day to day the little shoots grew and flourised till they were all well above the ground.

Then a terrible thing happened. One day, the men who were watering the crops saw a great number of crickets swarming over the ground nearest the mountains. As the crickets settled down they ate the tiny shoots and leaves to the ground. More came, and more, and ever more, till it was like an army of black, hopping, crawling crickets, streaming down the side of the mountain to kill the crops.

The men tried to kill the crickets by beating them down, but the numbers were so great that it was like beating at the sea. Then they ran and told the terrible news, and all the village came to help. They

started fires; they dug trenches and filled them with water; they ran wildly about in the fields, killing what they could. But while they fought in one place new armies of crickets marched down the mountainsides and attacked the fields in other places. And at last the people fell on their knees and prayed and wept and cried in despair, for they saw starvation and death in the fields.

Suddenly, from far off in the air toward the great salt lake, there was the sound of flapping wings. It grew louder. Some of the people looked up, startled. They saw, like a white cloud rising from the lake, a flock of seagulls flying toward them.

'The gulls! the gulls! was the cry. 'What does it mean?'

The gulls flew overhead, with a shrill chorus and then, in a marvellous white cloud of outspread wings, they settled down over the cultivated ground.

'Oh! no!'' cried the people. 'The gulls are eating what the crickets have left! they will strip root and branch!'

But all at once, someonce called out,

'But, see! they are eating the crickets! They are eating only the crickets!'

It was true. The gulls devoured the crickets in dozens, in hundreds, in swarms. And when at last they finished, they had stripped the fields of the army of crickets; and the people were saved.

To this day, in the beautiful city of Salt Lake, which grew out of that pioneer village, the children are taught to love the sea gulls. And when they learn drawing and weaving in the schools, their first design is often a picture of a cricket and a gull.

The Pardoner's Tale

(*Adapted from* The Canterbury Tales)

In the fourteenth century it was common for people to travel in groups to Canterbury Cathedral. It was believed that prayers would be speedily answered if made at the shrine of St Thomas á Becket, who was murdered there.

Chaucer's *Canterbury Tales* contains stories told by a group of such pilgrims as they travelled. Here is one of them retold. It is called 'The Three Rioters' or 'The Pardoner's Tale'.

Three young men were sitting in an inn early in the morning. Outside there came the sad sound of the hand bell that accompanied a coffin on its way to burial. One of the young men called the kitchen boy and asked him to run off and find out who it was that had died. The boy replied, 'I don't need to do that. I can already tell you. I think you knew him. He was drunk last night and died soon after. Death is everywhere now. He has killed a thousand local people in this present plague. You should be very careful, sirs. He is dangerous.'

The Innkeeper, who had been listening to the conversation, joined in, 'Why, yes, this boy speaks the truth. In a village not far from here he has killed every soul; man, woman, and child.'

The three young men were highly indignant. 'Why', they said, 'if the traitor Death is the cause of so much trouble we'll take a vow to kill him. Away with him as he has done away with all our friends.' And so they swore.

Drunk as they were, they got up and made their way towards the village they had been told of.

When they had walked awhile they met at a stile a very frail old man. They abused him, asking why he wasn't already dead and even accusing him of being a spy for Death. 'Tell us where Death is,' they taunted him, 'and we will let you go.'

The old man pointed them to a small grove of trees. 'There,' he said, 'I saw him there today.'

The three set off running for the trees, but imagine what should be their surprise when instead of Death they found heaps of gold pieces. Immediately, all thoughts of Death left their minds. Each of them began to think how he could get this treasure for himself. One, the youngest, went off to town to bring provisions. Secretly he planned to buy poison by which the other two would die.

The two left behind planned to kill the young man as soon as he returned. They said they would then share the treasure.

When the youngest returned, they killed him as they had planned. Then, well pleased with themselves, they each took a bottle of what they took to be wine and drank – and died – for what they drank was poison. Death had destroyed them by their own hands, through their own greed.

Rough Justice?

One Saturday evening in June, Farmer Phillips looked through his kitchen window across the fields to the road which ran up the hill to the village.

A car was parked by the gate which led to the field where Mr Phillips' dairy herd was grazing, and he noticed with alarm that the gate had been left open.

Mr Phillips put on his hat, grabbed his walking stick and, with an angry snort, he hurried across the field towards the parked car. He could see that a family of four had been picnicking in the field, and were now about to leave hurriedly. The man was calling to the two children to get into the car, and just before Mr Phillips arrived the car was already driving away. However, as Mr Phillips closed the gate he was just in time to read the registration number before it was out of sight.

Now the farmer was a kind man, and he had no objection to people from the towns visiting his farm to have picnics in his fields so long as they remembered to obey the Country Code. This tells everybody to close all gates, not to leave litter, not to pick wild flowers, and to see that farm animals and wildlife are not harmed in any way.

The family which had just left had behaved very badly. The farmer stood and prodded the grass with his stick where

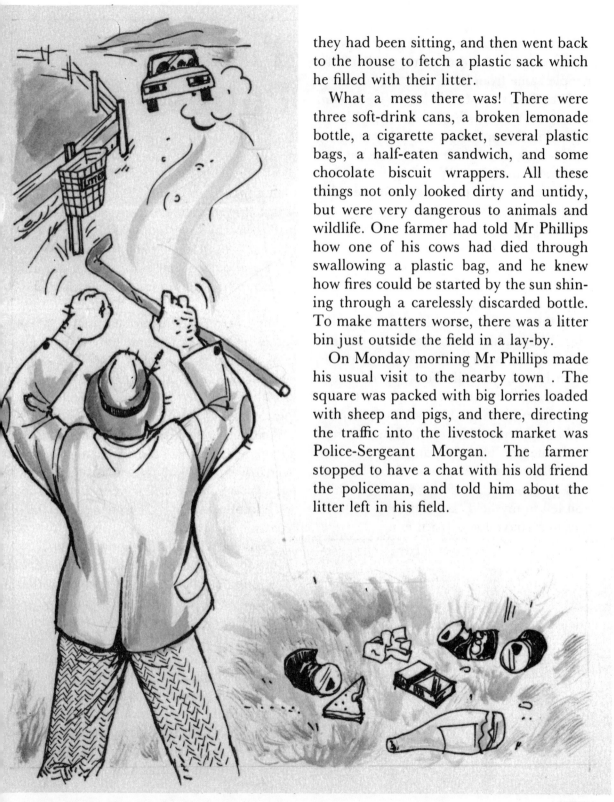

they had been sitting, and then went back to the house to fetch a plastic sack which he filled with their litter.

What a mess there was! There were three soft-drink cans, a broken lemonade bottle, a cigarette packet, several plastic bags, a half-eaten sandwich, and some chocolate biscuit wrappers. All these things not only looked dirty and untidy, but were very dangerous to animals and wildlife. One farmer had told Mr Phillips how one of his cows had died through swallowing a plastic bag, and he knew how fires could be started by the sun shining through a carelessly discarded bottle. To make matters worse, there was a litter bin just outside the field in a lay-by.

On Monday morning Mr Phillips made his usual visit to the nearby town . The square was packed with big lorries loaded with sheep and pigs, and there, directing the traffic into the livestock market was Police-Sergeant Morgan. The farmer stopped to have a chat with his old friend the policeman, and told him about the litter left in his field.

'I took the number of the car,' he said, 'but, of course, I don't know where the people came from.'

'Was it a red Morris?' asked Sergeant Morgan. 'You see, I noticed a red Morris parked in the square on Saturday morning and I took the number because the tax disc was out of date. Was this the number of the car?' The policeman showed Mr Phillips a number he had written in his notebook.

'Yes, it is,' said the farmer.

'Right, then,' said the policeman. 'I will find out the address from the vehicle registration office and let you know.'

So the next Saturday the farmer put the plastic bag in his car and set out to drive to the address which the policeman had given him. Eventually he stopped outside a modern house in a town about twenty miles from his farm. He took out the plastic bag and emptied it on the lawn in front of the house. Then he rang the doorbell, and when a man came to the door, he said:

'I've brought back these things which you left in my field last Saturday ˇ I think you must have forgotten them.''

The Lost Puppy

'Mummy, I can keep it, can't I? It was lost and followed me all the way home. I didn't call it or anything like that.'

Mrs Thornton looked down into the pleading eyes of her son. She sighed and wished with all her heart that it was possible.

'But Danny,' she replied gently. 'You know he belongs to somebody else. Probably a little boy just like you who's very sad because he thinks he has lost him. You wouldn't want to keep another little boy's puppy would you?'

Danny shook his head miserably. 'But Daddy did promise me one just before he went away. He said as soon as he got back we would go and look for one together.'

'I know, Danny.' She stroked his hair gently.

'Daddy will come home, won't he Mummy – one day he will come home?'

'I hope so dear, I hope and pray that one day he will come back to us.'

Tears misted her eyes as she hugged her son close to her. Six months ago her husband had kissed his son goodbye, promising to see him in a week's time. He had boarded his plane to the Middle East and had never returned. Enquiries had traced him to a town in Syria where he was known to have hired a jeep, but nothing more had been heard of him.

She continued to stroke her son's head absentmindedly, wondering for the thousandth time what could have happened to his father.

'You will take the little fellow to the police station, won't you dear?' she said softly

Danny wiped a tear away with his fist and nodded. Somehow he felt he owed it to his father not to worry her more if he could help it, so he picked the pup up and set off for the police station.

He explained to the constable behind the counter how he had found the puppy, and how it had followed him home. 'Sounds to me as if the puppy found you son. Hold on a tick while I fetch the lost property book. Must have all the particulars you know.'

Danny stared around him curiously as the constable disappeared into a back room. Then the door to his left opened, and policeman emerged, talking over his shoulder to somebody who was following him out.

'I will do my best, sir, but I can't promise anything. Of course, if central records can't help . . .'

A second man followed the policeman through the door. Danny stared. His mouth went dry. But the man was so pale, and so very thin. It couldn't be.

'Thank you so much for your help,' the second man replied.

'Daddy!' Danny's shout stopped both men in their tracks. 'Daddy,' he called again, and ran blindly to grasp the surprised man around the legs. His tear-stained face looking up desperately. The pale haggard man stared down at the

child, his face a deathly white. Slowly his eyes flickered in recognition.

'Danny?' he whispered. Then in a voice stronger, more sure, 'Danny!'

'Is this your father son?' the policeman enquired gently.

'Yes, yes, of course. Daddy, where have you been? Why didn't you come back to us?'

'I think you had both better come back into the office,' the inspector suggested as he ushered them back into the room.

Triggered by the recognition of Danny, Mr Thornton's memory began to return. It was patchy, but by teatime that day he was able to tell his wife that she had changed her hairstyle, and without any help from Danny had been able to find his way to his study. The doctor had called that afternoon, and assured them that in time his memory should return almost completely. Only the events leading up to the loss of memory might be lost for ever.

As that exciting day faded into dusk, Danny, who was staying up far beyond his normal bedtime, heard how his father had set off in a hired jeep to survey a site out in the desert. A storm had blown up and he remembered his jeep hitting a rock. He remembered nothing else until he woke up in hospital where he had been taken by Arabs who had found him cut and badly injured beside his stripped jeep. Even his clothes had been taken from him.

When he was well enough he had gone to the remains of the jeep and found, at the bottom of a plastic bag containing oily rags, a screwed-up receipt. He had been able to trace the receipt to a store in a local market town. For the last week he had been making enquiries in all the adjoining villages and towns. That was what he had been doing when Danny had found him.

There was a long silence. Finally, Danny spoke. 'I'm glad we didn't keep that puppy,' he said. His father squeezed him a little more tightly.

'Tomorrow we will go out and look for one together.'

'I've heard that before,' said Danny.

'Old Blocky'

Nobody ever knew how 'Old Blocky' came by his name. Very few people knew anything about him at all – where he came from or how he became a tramp. Nobody knew, nobody cared.

The moment he came into sight, young children would run to conceal themselves, and then, from the security of their hiding places, they would cup their hands to their mouths and shout in derision, 'Blocky, Old Blocky, Old Blockee!' Occasionally one of the older boys would throw a stone

before dashing back into hiding. Every so often this thin, grizzle-haired old man would slowly turn his weather-beaten face in the direction of his tormentors and wave his stick above his head.

Little Tommy Harris was only six but he had already learnt to run and hide himself whenever Old Blocky came into sight. Behind the wooden fence of his garden he would watch through a slit in the timber as this strange traveller shuffled past his home.

Friday night was pocket-money night. Tommy's father always came home early on Fridays, and as soon as he was settled in his armchair, Tommy would climb on to his knee. Sometimes his father would produce a coin from Tommy's hair or his ear. Sometimes he found one in Tommy's shoe or tucked away in his collar. Then, after promising to come straight back home, Tommy would be allowed to go to the corner shop to spend some of his money on sweets.

It was a sunny Friday afternoon. Tommy stood on tiptoe, engrossed. There were so many things to choose from. Bars of chocolate, packets of pastilles, wine-gums, all sorts of jelly animals. It was always like this, so very difficult to decide.

So absorbed was Tommy in making his choice that he didn't hear the slight shuffling sound behind him. A light tap on his shoulder startled him out of his thoughts. He turned and found himself staring up into the face of Old Blocky. For a second he stood paralysed with fear as the old tramp stood there with one arm outstretched. Two peanuts in their shells rested on his twisted and gnarled hand.

Then Tommy cried in terror, dropped the two coins he had been clutching and fled for home.

Strangely enough, after he had been comforted by his parents and gently put to bed, he found himself thinking calmly about this strange old man. He remembered the blue eyes set deeply in the stubbly face. He remembered how they had twinkled almost as if he had been smiling, and the expression on his face. It had seemed kindly, almost loving.

Next morning he was even more puzzled, for as he opened the front door to fetch the morning paper for his father there, lying on the doorstep, were his two coins . . .

Many years later, when Tommy was grown up and had almost forgotten about Old Blocky, he learnt a little about the old tramp. He was visiting his aunt and she made the comment that one no longer saw tramps in the numbers one used to. This made Tommy recall Old Blocky, and he told his aunt of his encounter with the old man.

'Why,' said his aunt, 'you are talking about poor old Sam Roots. A remarkably kind and gentle person he was, too. Poor old Sam. Married the wrong woman of course.'

'He was married?' exclaimed Tommy.

'He was. As far as I know he remained married until the day he passed away. They seemed a very happy couple, too, when I first knew them. They ran the village shop. My mother was always sending me there to buy odd bits and pieces. Sam would often dip into a jar and find me a sweet. Then came the war, and he was one of the first to go. By this time, they had a lovely little baby girl. Sam absolutely worshipped her. Well, it was the old story – he stopped receiving letters from his wife. When he finally arrived home, she had gone. Taken the baby with her, of course. The shop was in ruins, and no word to anybody as to where she had gone. Poor Sam. People tried to persuade him to reopen the shop and rebuild his life, but he had to find his child. So he set off to look for her. And I suppose in a way he spent the rest of his days searching for her. It's my belief she took the baby overseas, but Sam never gave up hope or lost his love of children.'

Tommy felt sad as he heard the story and remembered how cruel he and the rest of his playmates had been.

'Why were we so unkind to him?' he murmured to himself. 'We must have hurt him cruelly.'

'Why?' his aunt repeated. 'For the same reason people have always been cruel to other people. Because he was different, because he didn't conform. Because he was judged by his appearance and because people didn't understand.'

The Three Frogs

In the little market town of Tadcombe the villagers were used to seeing frogs hopping around the lily ponds, the marshes and the river banks. Why they had so many frogs in that particular village nobody ever knew, but they didn't cause too much of a nuisance. Except, that is, for three particular frogs who somehow seemed different. They were very adventurous and sometimes very mischevous and were always being found in the most unlikely and inconvenient places. Some children had found them in their school bags; mothers had seen them hopping in and out of lar-

ders, and someone had once found them sleeping cosily in his bed!

The frogs had very different personalities. The first frog was lazy and complacent. Whenever he did anything he used the very least amount of energy and always assumed that if he was in a fix someone else would help him out. He had lots of friends, however, because many of the other frogs thought his easy attitude to everything was quite fun.

The second frog was rather a bully. He always forced the other frogs to help him when he was in trouble or wanted something done. He was very crafty and often cruel.

The third frog was different again. He always tried hard at whatever he did and made the most of any situation without complaining too much and without harming the other frogs.

One warm summer's day, the three frogs felt very hot and sticky and they hopped around trying to find somewhere cool and pleasant to relax. They made their way into the local farmer's house, because there were always interesting things going on at the farm. They hopped into her kitchen and suddenly saw that the larder door was open. The larder would be well stocked with food as well as being nice and cool. In they hopped. They were even more excited when they saw a huge bowl of cream on one of the shelves. An ideal swimming pool in which to cool off!

The first frog leapt in happily – followed by the second who, because he was a bully, pushed the third frog in first before he dived in. They all swam around contentedly, but after a few minutes they began to tire. The cream was very thick and it was much more difficult to swim than they had expected.

The first frog just gave up trying and slowly sank to the bottom. The second one, realising the danger, lashed out with his long legs and tried to stand on the third frog's back so that he could leap to safety, but he slipped and he, too, sunk to the bottom of the bowl. The third frog continued swimming for all he was worth, putting every ounce of energy into keeping afloat. He swam and swam, whipping the cream into a lather, but he did not seem to move very far. Suddenly he felt something solid near his back legs – he thought it was the side of the bowl but it couldn't be for he was still in the middle. Then he realised what was happening. The cream all around him was slowly turning into butter from all the whisking and lashing of his legs. Very, very slowly he made his way to safety. He hadn't given up, and his perseverance and effort had been justly rewarded.

Second Thoughts

'This is great!' Mark told himself. He hadn't been a swimmer for long, and now, quite suddenly, he found himself speeding through the water like a professional. 'I never knew it could be so easy,' he thought. It was almost the last day of camp. Tomorrow he thought he would be going home. They had been kicking a rubber ball around the beach. A strong miskick from Gerry had sent it soaring into the waves and Mark, being nearest, had plunged in after it. Despite his new-found speed, the ball continued to keep a tantalising distance in front of him. Made confident by his success he put in an extra effort and found himself at last alongside the ball. Triumphantly he grabbed at it and at the same time tried to turn in the water. Then it happened. It was as if somebody or something was holding his legs under the water. Desperately he abandoned the ball and tried to strike out with his arms. His legs just wouldn't come up. Something seemed to be dragging him down. The sea closed over his head. Sudden realisation came to him: 'I'm drowning!' Surprise and bewilderment kept off fear. His hand and then his head broke the water. On the beach he could see his friends who seemed to be waving at him. How far away they seemed! Could he really have swum that far? How could his

brother go home and tell his mother he was drowned? Somehow the thought made him feel guilty as the sea again closed over his head. A thousand memories flooded his brain: his first tricycle; Father carrying him on his shoulders to the circus; Mother nursing him when he had been so ill; his first proper birthday party; and the time, so long ago now, when he had broken one of Mother's favourite flowers in the garden and propped up the stalk with the aid of a stick so that Mother wouldn't notice it. Why was he remembering this now? Strangely, he felt ashamed about it and sorry, so very sorry. Now he was drowning – too late to say sorry or thank you – too late . . .

He was aware of water gushing from his mouth, he couldn't breathe. He felt water coming up from deep inside of him, almost like a pump. He gasped for air. He was aware of the sharp sand on his face. Somebody was sitting on his back, and his ears seemed to be blocked, but he was vaguely aware of voices around him.

'He's coming round!'

'Thank God!'

'Mark! Mark!' He recognised the voice of his brother. It was as if he was pleading. He tried to turn his head, felt salt-water and sand in his mouth, and tried to spit it out.

'Sit him up!' Gentle hands turned him and held him up. He sat with his arms extended behind him gasping for air. 'I couldn't get my stroke,' he explained.

'You idiot! You were warned of the current.' John was obviously getting over his fright.

Suddenly Mark realised. He wasn't such a wonderful swimmer after all. It was the current that had carried both the ball and him out to sea.

'What happened – how did I get out? I thought I was drowned.'

'Skipper was right behind you. He just managed to grab you and drag you out. We were all shouting at you to come back . . .'

In the weeks that followed, Mark often recalled his experience. The memory of the flower in the garden had been so vivid. It had happened so long ago – he could only have been about four or five. He had done many worse things since – why, he wondered, should this particular incident stay in his brain.

Gradually, over the months, the whole thing faded into the back of his mind. He was soon to go to university, and the scout camp of two years ago seemed a long way away.

He had a problem. His favourite rock star, Lance Cordell, was performing at the Globe. He had promised to go with his friends Steven, Sue and Anne. Anne was rather special, so although he couldn't afford the cost of the ticket, the combination of Anne and Lance Cordell was too good to pass up.

Standing in front of the metal cigarette box he wished he didn't feel so rotten. The box contained the money that his parents had put aside to help purchase the books and equipment he would need when he went to university. It was money he knew his mother and father could ill afford. It represented months of sacrifice and going without. He opened the box. After all, he was only really borrowing a few pounds. One day he would make it up to them. He thought of Lance Cordell – and Anne – then the picture of a small boy propping up a flower with a twig came into his mind. It must have been the first time he had tried to deceive his Mother. He dropped the money back into the box. He would 'phone Steven and say he couldn't come.

Risks

It was a November evening in 1943. I stood at the bus stop in the Midland industrial city. I felt very smart in my best naval uniform, and even the blackout and the threat of another air raid was not enough to keep me indoors. After all, this was likely to be the last opportunity for me to be at home on leave for a long, long time, and I wanted to visit as many of my friends and relatives as I could.

The bus finally arrived, and I stepped up on to the platform. The conductor took my money and, by the dim light of the partially blacked-out torch, always pointing downwards, he removed my ticket from the hand-held rack and clipped it into the metal clipper at his hip. I made my way inside the bus and sat down at an empty seat in the dimly lit vehicle. As I sat down, the unmistakable wail of the air-raid warning siren began to drone out across the city. I glanced around me. There were about half a dozen other people on the bus, factory workers, men and women, on their way to the local munitions factory for a twelve-hour night-shift. They took little notice of the siren. After all, this was part of their lives. It happened nearly every night.

It seemed only minutes before the deep thud of the anti-aircraft guns could be felt, each one seeming to shake the earth as the bus moved slowly and rather uncertainly along the road to the city centre. The distinctive, intermittent drone of enemy bombers became apparent, interspersed with the more continuous hum of our own fighter aircraft racing to intercept.

We were approaching a well-known road junction near the centre of the city when there was a piercing scream through the air, a tremendous shaking of the ground, like an earthquake, and the bus shuddered to an abrupt halt.

After a hurried consultation with the driver, the conductor stepped up onto the gangway and said, 'Landmine! At the crossroads! It's hit a gas main. We can't go any further. You'll all have to get off.'

Slowly, the small group of people dismounted from the stricken vehicle, the smell of smoke and burning debris all around. A short distance in front of us was a tall sheet of flame, where the bomb had ignited the fractured gas main. The heat was almost unbearable.

As I stood hesitating, watching the terrifying flame, uncertain what to do, I heard a voice at my side. 'This way. Down here. Away from the main road.'

I turned and looked at my companion. He was a small man, about fifty or sixty years of age, I guess. It was difficult to tell. His hair was grey, as was his moustache, although that was stained brown at one side, probably through taking snuff. He carried a blue enamel can, with his hot drink inside, and a small metal case that probably contained sandwiches.

'Down this way. The side road.'

I allowed him to lead me away from the devastation, away from pieces of shrapnel from the anti-aircraft guns spattering around us.

Suddenly, we heard another piercing

scream and we both knew what that meant. Without realising what was happening, I found myself flung to the ground, face downwards, my companion spread-eagled across my body, to protect me, his metal case above my head. The screaming stopped. There was a split-second's silence, followed by a shattering explosion and violent convulsions of the pavement beneath us. The air was filled with dust, making breathing an effort. Gradually the dust subsided and we could hear the drone of aircraft fading into the distance.

We stood up, dusting down our filthy clothing as best we could. I gazed at my companion.

'That was close,' was all he said.

'You risked your life for me,' I gasped. 'You could have been killed.'

'Gotta look after you blokes,' he replied. 'You've gotta fight a war.'

He stood staring at me for a few moments before he said, 'You're only a babby.'

'I'm eighteen,' I protested, feeling very adult.

He smiled slightly. 'Like I said – only a babby. Well, I'd best get along and see if the factory's still there. After all, there's a war on.'

He walked off into the darkness, chuckling quietly to himself as if enjoying a private joke.

Actually, the factory *was* still there, it had escaped damage. But seven nights later, the night before I was due to join my ship, it did not escape. About two-thirds of the factory was destroyed, and there were hundreds of dead and injured.

I've often wondered about the little man with the stained moustache. I hope he survived and lived to a ripe old age. He deserved that as much as any man I've ever met.

Envy

David Aintrey gave the punchball a last furious flurry of punches then sank back on his bed exhausted. He gazed at himself in the mirror. The face that scowled back at him reflected the frustration and despair that had been clouding his mind for many months. Despite all his efforts, he remained just 1.5 metres tall, the shortest boy in the fifth form. How he longed to mix with his classmates on equal terms instead of being an oddity, always on the outside.

He thought with envy of 'Jumbo' Burrows, captain of the school soccer team and 1.8 metres tall at least, and 'Red' Leather who wasn't much shorter. There were dozens of others taller than David. He envied them all for being 'normal'.

On Thursday morning David was making his way to his locker, passing a group of boys clustered around the notice board.

'Hey Dainty, you're in the school team for Saturday's match.'

David stopped. Were they fooling about with him again? With a thumping heart he walked back to the notice board.

'There you are. D. Aintrey, number seven. Old Tomlinson has put you in in place of Roger Platt. About time, too, he was no use anyway.'

Somebody patted his back. He was being noticed, accepted. Good wishes and congratulations were coming from all sides. He was in the school team. He glowed with pride. 'Wait till I tell Dad,' he thought.

The day of the match arrived at last, and at half past ten, self-conscious in the school strip, he followed his team-mates on to the pitch. He tried not to look at the handful of spectators gathered on the touchline.

Half-time came with no score.

Most of the second half followed the pattern of the first, and both teams' defenders prevented any real scoring chances. The final whistle was very close when Taffy Davis put a long cross from the left wing almost at David's feet. Instantly David was running the ball into an empty space to his right. A hefty defender loomed over him, but David's small wiry frame swerved inside of him and he was away. Another red shirt was converging on him. It had to be now. With his left foot he drove a high curving shot to the left. It sailed past the outstretched hands of the 'keeper and into the net.

Half a dozen hands thumped him on the back.

'Good old Dainty.'

'Well done, David old son.'

From the touchline Mr. Tomlinson's voice boomed. 'Good shot Aintrey. Well played lad.'

The ball had barely been put into play again when the final whistle sounded. David's goal had won the match.

For David, the walking off the field, the shower and the changing room were pure magic. All he had ever dreamt of, all he had ever wanted, was happening for him.

In the dressing room, David suddenly noticed that Jumbo, seated on a high box was holding a handrolled cigarette to his lips. He puffed at it a few times before handing it to Taffy Davis. David caught a whiff of the smoke. It was sweeter, different to most tobaccos. Suddenly David realised. They were smoking pot.

Jumbo caught sight of him on the fringe of the group.

'Hey! What about our match winner. He hasn't had a draw yet. Red, hand that weed over to young Dainty there.' Jumbo's speech seemed slurred, his eyes squinted. There was a foolish grin on his face. A strange feeling of disappointment in seeing Jumbo like this made David feel rather flat for the first time that afternoon.

'No thanks, I, er, don't.'

Immediately a chorus of protest swelled up from the rest of the team.

'Come on Dainty, it won't hurt you.'

'Hey man, you're one of us now. You've got to have a smoke.'

David knew that if he wanted to remain one of them he had to join in. A couple of

puffs wasn't going to do any harm, surely? Then he thought again and remembered all the warnings he had had from his parents and friends. Sadly he shook his head.

'Chicken! You're chicken, man.'

Stubbornly David shook his head and turned to go. As he passed the lockers he felt himself in collision with someone. It was Mr. Tomlinson!

On Monday morning they all stood in a line in front of the Head's desk.

'My secretary is typing a letter to each of your parents and I am suspending each of you for two weeks.'

'Please Sir?'

'What is it, Long? Have you something to say for yourself at last?'

'Please Sir, about Daint . . . I mean David Aintrey, Sir.'

'What about David Aintrey?'

'He didn't take a smoke Sir. He wouldn't.'

'Is this true?'

A mumbled assent came from the row of boys.

'Very well, Aintrey. You may go. At least one of you has some sense.'

David waited in the corridor for the rest of the team to file out. They looked pale and shaken. He went over to Tim Long.

'Tim, I wanted to thank you. You know, for speaking up for me in there.'

Tim grinned at him weakly, 'That's alright. Only fair, after all. Anyway, it took real guts to stand there and refuse their reefers. I wish I had had your guts.'

An African Gift

Yewande the young African girl listened carefully as the teacher explained why it is that Christians give presents to each other on Christmas Day.

'The gift is an expression of our joy over the birth of Jesus, and our friendship for each other,' the teacher said.

When Christmas Day came, Yewande brought the teacher a sea shell of lustrous beauty. 'Wherever did you find such a beautiful shell?' the teacher asked, as she gently fingered the gift.

Yewande told her that there was only one spot where such extraordinary shells could be found. When she named the place, Kumalo, a picturesque bay some six kilometres away, the teacher was left speechless.

'Why. . . . it's gorgeous. . . . wonderful, but you shouldn't have gone all that way to get a gift for me.'

With her eyes brightening, Yewande smiled and answered slowly, 'The long walk was part of the gift.'

Thanks

During the Second World War many lives were saved by the men and women of the Civil Defence. The wardens, rescue men, ambulance workers and stretcher parties were often volunteers who worked during the day at civilian jobs and reported each night for duties.

Billy and Frank were two such volunteers. They were much younger than most of the men on the station, and had something of a reputation as practical jokers.

One of the stretcher party men was a professional artist who had recently completed a sketch of the station superintendent. Unfortunately Billy and Frank had got their hands on it and were busy framing it in a spare toilet seat they had found. 'A thing of beauty is a joy forever,' Frank murmured as he carefully painted red roses around the frame.

'Where are we going to hang this lovely thing?' Billy enquired.

'I suggest the dining room. We can change one clock for another.'

They waited until midnight and then made their way stealthily to the canteen with the framed portrait. Billy climbed up and passed the clock down to Frank, who handed up the frame. They were standing back admiring their handiwork when the air-raid siren wailed. Almost immediately nearby anti-aircraft guns opened up. As they ran for their steel helmets and gas-masks, the building was shaken by heavy bombs falling in the vicinity. Around

them, men who had been sleeping on stretchers awoke and reached for their tunics and helmets. The telephone rang, and in seconds the Civil Defence teams were speeding to their destination.

As they drove through the London suburbs, shells burst overhead and the occasional thump of a bomb could be clearly heard – sometimes felt. Soon the car was bumping over debris that had been flung across the road, and they knew they were nearing their destination.

As Billy and Frank and the others piled out of the cars they could see the wide, black space in the row of terraced houses

where two or three houses had stood a few minutes ago. Two lorries arrived and disgorged their complement of rescue workers, closely followed by a doctor. Casualties were already awaiting attention, and for the next forty-five minutes the rescue parties were busy with the dead and injured, applying bandages and splints where needed and loading stretchers into ambulances. When all the casualties had been attended, Frank walked over to where a group had congregated by a house that had only partly been demolished. The rescue squad had made the usual form of entry by tunnelling through the base of the rubble at floor level, shoring up the sides with scaffolding. This provided a passage less than a metre wide and approximately half a metre high. They had reported an injured woman in the back room.

'Why the devil didn't you try to get to her?' the doctor demanded.

'Too risky mate. Could have had the whole lot on top of us.'

'Well, it *is* your job,' a warden pointed out.

'Don't see that – she needed first aid for sure. I reckon it's up to the ambulance service or the doctor.' The doctor looked distinctly uneasy. Bill looked at Frank and raised an eyebrow. Frank nodded and began to take off his gas-mask. Billy was first to the tunnel, followed by Frank.

They crawled slowly on their stomachs, trying to protect their eyes from the constant fall of dust and plaster. Above and around them timbers creaked and groaned ominously. Once or twice they froze as a slithering and sliding above threatened to bury them alive. At last they reached the end of the tunnel. It opened into what had been a living room in the back of the house. A huge timber now blocked their path.

'Listen!' Billy hissed. They both listened. At first they heard only the creaking timbers above them. Then they heard the unmistakeable whimper of a baby. 'Good Lord, we've got to try to do something,' exclaimed Billy. Slowly he began to move bricks and rubble from above the beam at the end which rested on the floor, to try and make room to wriggle through to where the sound was coming from. At last a hole was cleared.

'I'm going through,' Billy announced. Slowly, very gingerly, he wriggled his head and shoulders through. Frank helped lift his legs so that he could move forward on his hands until his body was clear of the hole. Frank's torch beam quickly located the body of a young woman lying beside a cupboard. A wooden rafter was across her body. Billy reached over the woman, then stood up. Frank saw that he was holding a young baby in his hands. 'Congratulations!' grinned Billy. 'We have a bouncing baby boy.' He carried the baby to where Frank waited at the tunnel entrance. 'Hang on,' he said. 'I think his mother is still alive.'

The cupboard had taken the weight of the beams, and Billy had little difficulty in pulling the woman clear. He dragged her to where Frank waited. Carefully they manoeuvred the woman through the gap. Frank, lying on his back, placed his hands under the woman's arms and, very slowly and carefully, dragged her backwards. Billy, one arm holding the baby protectively, gave what aid he could. They moved slowly back for what seemed an eternity, when suddenly strong hands grabbed Frank's legs and eased him to safety and fresh air. Within a few minutes things came into focus again. Somebody handed him a mug of tea. Through a swirling mist he saw his friend, face black, eyes as red-rimmed as his own, clothes torn and filthy. Billy sauntered over. 'Piece of cake,' he announced.

That evening, they were both summoned to the superintendent's office. The superintendent glared at them from under heavy eyebrows as they entered. 'There is a little matter of a toilet seat,' he hissed, 'and a clock removed from the canteen. You will get the clock up and the toilet seat down, and I want no more monkey business from you two.'

'Right, sir,' Billy answered.

'There's another thing I want to say to you two,' said the superintendent. 'I've been hearing of your antics this morning – that woman and child you dragged out. They'll never know who got them out, but because of what you did they will go on living. Well, since they won't be able to say thank you, and as I suppose it was worth a couple of words of thanks, I'm saying it for them.'

The superintendent, for once his frosty glare turning to a warm grin, stood up and shook their hands vigorously.

The Mystery of the Dogon Tribe

Deep in the heart of Africa in the country of Mali, near the Sahara Desert, lives the Dogon tribe. The Dogons are remarkable for the fact that their most sacred beliefs are founded on a star called Sirius B. For hundreds of years this star has played a most important role in their lives. They know it has an elliptical orbit. They know its position within the orbit, and they know it is unusually heavy.

But here is the mystery. The existence of the star was not even guessed at by Western astronomers until the middle of the last century. It is invisible to the naked eye and was photographed for the first time in 1970. Where then, did the Dogons get their knowledge? Well, if you ask them they will tell you that visitors from Sirius B landed on earth hundreds of years ago and described their planet to the Dogons. Ask what the visitors looked like, and the Dogons will describe them as Nommos (or amphibians). They tell how they arrived in a ship or ark which was spurting blood from its tail, (perhaps they mean the exhaust from a rocket?). They also tell of a big star that stayed in the sky when the Nommos landed.

All this might be dismissed as nonsense,

Lost

David sat back in his uncle's Lincoln and thought of the events of the past week of his holiday. The trip up the tallest tower in the world where he had looked over Toronto and beyond while his cousin had pointed out the sights. The day spent at Toronto Place where he had seen that marvellous three-dimensional film of the Rocky Mountains and forest fires. He remembered feeling dizzy looking down at the raging waters at the Niagara Falls, the visits to the pioneer village and Fort York. It had all been wonderful. Now he was leaving Toronto behind to stay at his uncle's summer cottage at the lakes. He turned to his older brother Jonathan who was sitting beside him. 'When do you think we will see the Indians?' His uncle had promised that there were Indians living near the lakes.

Jonathan, who at fourteen was nearly four years older, tried to act grown up these days.

'You'll see them soon enough,' he said in his newly acquired condescending air. Their uncle turned from the front seat and grinned at them.

'In just about ten minutes we'll pay a call on them if you like.' David's eyes widened. 'Really?' was all he could say.

As the car slowed down, David eagerly pressed his nose to the window. In the centre of an asphalted courtyard stood a totem pole. To the back of the asphalt were two or three timber buildings dis-

but a closer study of the Dogon tribe reveals that the people came originally from Libya. The Babylonians, who lived in the same area as the first Dogons, also had an amphibian God named Oannes. He is said to have taught the Sumerians astronomy, mathematics, and how to sow and reap. He had even given them a language.

What is the answer to this riddle? Why does a remote tribe in Africa have such unusual knowledge? Has this world once been visited by a strange civilisation?

playing leather articles and momentos for sale. They climbed out of the car to study the mocassins, beaded belts, head-bands and model tepees displayed. David looked up at his uncle. 'Where are the Indians?' he whispered. His uncle nodded to the attendants in the shops. '*They* are Indians,' he laughed.

As they climbed back into the car to resume their journey, David expressed his disappointment. 'They looked just like ordinary people,' he complained.

'They are ordinary people, you idiot!' his older brother informed him. 'They gave up plaiting their hair and wearing head-dresses years ago.'

They continued their journey for another two hours, over highways, down tracks and finally by boat across a large lake – the only way to get to their holiday cottage.

The first two days the boys spent fishing and swimming. Once they watched a seaplane land on the lake. Their uncle told them it belonged to people on the other side of the lake. Apart from this they saw nobody. The neighbouring cottages about a kilometre away on either side of them were deserted.

It had been arranged that their uncle, who had business in Toronto, would leave them for a couple of days. He had spent two days instructing them, insisting that they wear life-jackets in the boat, showing them how they could walk around the shoreline, and warning them never to go out of sight of the cottage. The forest reached right down to the water line. 'Walk twenty steps out of sight of the cottage and you could be lost forever', he warned.

The third morning they watched their uncle speed off in the cabin cruiser, and settled down to check their fishing tackle.

As they worked, David noticed a small movement on the steps by the cottage. 'Look', he whispered to Jonathan.

'It's a chipmunk – let's see if we can get closer.' But every time they got close it darted further away. The boys followed, and were within touching distance of it when it scampered off once again.

Suddenly the boys looked around them and remembered their uncle's warning. 'Walk twenty steps from the cottage and you could be lost forever.'

'We go this way,' David suggested, only slightly confidently. But everything seemed unfamiliar. 'We're lost, aren't we?' There was a tremor in David's voice.

Jonathan looked at his younger brother. He saw fears filling David's eyes. He crossed over and put his arms around him. 'Don't worry, Davey boy. We'll be alright.' Together they sat on a rocky outcrop, Jonathan thinking hard, David looking up into his brother's face hopefully.

The whole afternoon and evening was spent waiting and listening, but it was all in vain.

Slowly the heat left the day. The boys were wearing only shorts and light t-shirts. They made a makeshift shelter and slept fitfully, very afraid in the dark. The next day was a repeat of the first. They spoke to each other less and less.

The sun was gently piercing the shelter that evening when Jonathan felt a tug on his shoulder and a deep, strange voice saying 'Come'. He turned to see a swarthy face surrounded by blue-black hair. An Indian. They were safe.

Driving past the Indian shops at the end of their holiday, their uncle turned around to David. 'Well, what do you think of the Indians now?'

David glowed with enthusiasm. 'Magic,' he said. 'They may not wear feathers any longer, but they are still fantastic trackers!'

Oliver's Birthday

Oliver found it hard to be patient, despite his mother's plea. It was his birthday, and he wanted to spend some of the money that he had been sent by Uncle Sid. At last his mother was ready to go to the shops in the town.

Once they were there his mother suggested that Oliver went to look at the toys in Tomkins, the big department store, while she did the bits of shopping she had on her list. 'I'll meet you outside Tomkins in fifteen minutes,' Oliver's mother said. Oliver thought they were really crafty at Tomkins. When you went in you started at the cheap end with the biros, rubbers and rulers, penknives and paints, and then suddenly you zoomed to the expensive end with cameras, roller skates, electric trains and computers. He decided to buy a penknife with his money. And then he saw it. . . . an instant camera! 'That's what I want,' he thought. 'I could take pictures of all my friends.'

'Hello Oliver,' He looked up. It was Mary Martin, the shop assistant. Mary used to be his baby-sitter, years ago, when he was about two. 'You've just arrived at the right moment. I've left my handbag in the powder room. Just keep an eye on things. You can't trust anyone these days. I'll only be a couple of minutes.' Oliver's thoughts went back to the camera. His hand reached out, picked it up and pushed it under his T-shirt. He thrust his left hand into his anorak pocket and pulled it round out of sight.

'Have I been missed?' Mary was back. 'Did anyone want me?' 'No, only me,' Oliver replied. 'How much is your cheapest computer?' He thought he was being clever, taking her attention away from the camera section. Oliver suddenly realised that Mary was going to be in awful trouble when the manager discovered that a camera was missing. Fear gripped his inside. He mumbled something about meeting his mother. The camera was slipping. It would crash on the floor. He pushed his right hand up his T-shirt, grabbed the camera and slipped it in the right-hand pocket of his anorak.

Mother was waiting for him outside Tomkins. 'Come along Oliver. You are late. Have you bought something nice?' 'A penknife,' he said, 'the kind I've always wanted.'

When they reached home his mother went into the house and he wandered down to the trees at the bottom of the garden. No-one could see him. He stood still. Very slowly he took the camera out of his anorak. He couldn't stop thinking about Mary and wondered whether she would lose her job. Jobs were hard to get. He hated the camera. It was useless. He wanted to get rid of it, but there was nowhere to put it. The houses all around looked dead, but he felt that unseen people were watching him from behind their curtains.

As he was going upstairs to his room he heard his father's car in the drive. There was only one place to hide the camera and that was in the wardrobe. He opened the door and pushed it under a pile of clothes. The hollow feeling in the pit of his stomach was making him feel sick. He was feeling hot.

His mother called from downstairs, 'Oliver, are you coming downstairs? It's your birthday party! Get a move on!' He went downstairs. As he pushed open the dining room door he saw, to his horror, that the camera was on the table standing in front of the birthday cake. The camera that he had just hidden in the bottom of his wardrobe!

He blurted out, 'Yes, I took it. I stole it.'

His father said, 'What on earth are you talking about? Aren't you pleased with it? It's your birthday present from your mother and me. Oliver shrank away from the camera.

'I took it from the counter. I stole it from Tomkins,' he blurted out. At that moment his mother said, 'There's a policeman coming up the drive.'

The front doorbell rang. 'There's been a lot of shoplifting in the town,' the policeman said. 'Most of the large department stores like Tomkins have installed security devices. Could it be possible that your son was in Tomkins this morning? They have a video . . . a boy in a red T-shirt . . . green anorak . . . removing a camera . . .' Oliver's father turned angrily to him and said, 'And what have you got to say about this, young man?'

Of course Oliver was punished. It was a long time before he recovered from the guilt and shame and the awful ache deep inside him. That aching feeling is called

our conscience, and we feel it telling us whenever we do wrong. After the episode with the camera, Oliver started to listen a little more often to his conscience.

Appointment at Samara

However large and frightening they may be, it is never worthwhile to run away from one's problems and difficulties, as this story shows.

Ibn Seyd was a brave, old, Arabian war-leader with most of his great exploits already far in the past when, one day, he sent for his servant and told him to go to the market-place and buy food. The servant had not been away for more than a few minutes before he returned empty-handed and breathless. From the distraught look on his face, he was thoroughly alarmed, almost incoherent with panic and visibly shaking. It took Ibn Seyd some little time to learn from him what happened.

'My Lord,' the servant said. 'As you bade me I went quickly to the market-place to buy food and when I was almost there, I saw a ghastly figure, with his cloak acrosss his face. As I came near he drew this aside revealing two staring eyes set in a dead-white face. Master, I saw that it was indeed Death who confronted me and as I ran past him he raised his hand as if to strike me. Please, master, give me leave to go away from here before he attacks me again, and I will cross the desert to Samara to seek refuge with my brother.'

Ibn Seyd was a kindly man and, seeing that his servant was petrified with fear, freely gave him permission as he had asked, and the servant straightway left for Samara.

Then Ibn Seyd himself went down to the market-place to buy his food. On the way there, he, too, saw the same gaunt stranger with his cloak covering most of his face and with only his ghastly, staring eyes showing. Ibn, however, had faced Death too often on the battlefield to be afraid of him now. Therefore, he went boldly up to him and, looking him steadily in the face, said calmly,

'Death, as you know, I have become acquainted with you for a long time, and have met you on many a field of battle since, when I was still young I first took up arms. I have never feared you, and do not fear you now. Why then do you not reserve your anger for men like me rather than lift your hand against my poor servant who has never harmed a single person, let alone you?'

As their eyes met, Death replied just a firmly,

As you say, Ibn Seyd, we have long been acquainted and at many a place of slaughter you have outfaced me. Believe me, then, when I say that I did not raise my hand to strike your servant, but put it up only in surprise at seeing him here. For God had charged me with a mission and before the end of tomorrow I am bidden lay my hands on your servant in Samara, a long way from here.'

Sunset for Sale

(*Adapted from* Titus Alone *by Mervyn Peake*)

The stranger sat at a corner table in a street café. As far as one could see in either direction along the straight street were similar cafés. It wasn't a very prosperous area for all that. The people who sat, two here, three there, were poorly dressed and had a ragged, listless air about them. Those near enough to be able to see the stranger were showing a great deal of interest in him. He was a big man with a large hooked nose and long hair. A number of people were staring at him unashamedly. Strangers, it seems, were rare.

A small, bent, old man dressed in black was threading his way through the tables on the street. His wrinkled head protruded from his torn collar. His eyes were black and beady. Every now and then he threw back his head and barked out, 'Buy it. Buy it. A seat for the sunset. They say it will be coral, green and grey. Twenty pence, only twenty pence!'

When he came upon the stranger the old man paused. He opened his mouth but was silent with surprise. At last he began again, 'A seat for the sunset, sir? Two pence for the standing. Three pence for the sitting. One penny in the trees. Buy it up. Buy. Buy. Buy.' He thrust his tickets at the stranger.

voice. 'The green will be like grass. To-night, coral, green and grey.'

It is so often the case in life that the things we pay nothing for we tend to take for granted. If we did have to pay, how much more we would appreciate the sunset!'

'What does he mean?' mumbled the stranger to himself. 'do we have to pay to see the sunset now? Ain't the sunset free? Good God, ain't even the sunset free?'

'It's all we have,' said a voice. 'That, and the dawn.'

The ticket-seller leaned over the stranger. 'Free, did you say?' he said. 'How *could* it be free. With such wondrous colours, fit for a queen. Isn't there nothing sacred? Buy a chair Mr Giant and see it comfortable. Buy. Thank you, sir. Thank you. For *you* the *cedar* benches sir.'

'What happens if the wind changes?' asked the stranger. 'Do I get my money back?'

'Tonight there is no wind,' said another

Thematic Index